CURRICULUM REFORM
in the
ELEMENTARY SCHOOL

Creating Your Own Agenda

CURRICULUM REFORM
in the
ELEMENTARY SCHOOL

Creating Your Own Agenda

M. FRANCES KLEIN

Foreword by John I. Goodlad

Teachers College, Columbia University
New York and London

Published by Teachers College Press, 1234 Amsterdam Avenue,
New York, NY 10027

Library of Congress Cataloging-in-Publication Data

Klein, M. Frances.
    Curriculum reform in the elementary school : creating your own
agenda / M. Frances Klein ; foreword by John I. Goodlad.
        p.   cm.
    Bibliography: p.
    Includes index.
    ISBN 0-8077-2940-X.   ISBN 0-8077-2939-6 (pbk.)
    1. Elementary school administration — United States.   2. Curriculum
planning — United States.   3. Curriculum change — United States.
4. School improvement programs — United States.   I. Title.
LB2822.5.K54 1989   88-29487
372.19'0973 — dc19   CIP

ISBN 0-8077-2940-X
ISBN 0-8077-2936-6 (pbk.)

Manufactured in the United States of America

94   93   92   91   90   89   1   2   3   4   5   6

Contents

Foreword, *by John I. Goodlad*   vii

Preface   xi

**1 Overview: Process and Substance
    of Curriculum Reform**   **1**

Reform at the Local Level   3

Organizing for Change   5

Getting Started and Maintaining Momentum   9

Summary   11

2 The Intended Curriculum   **13**

Surveying the Educative Functions of Schooling   14

Analysis of Curriculum Guides   24

Selection of Content and Learning Materials   29

Sources of Influence Over Instructional Content   34

Issues to Be Considered in the Intended Curriculum   38

3 Classroom Practices   **46**

How Time Was Spent   47

Instructional Practices Used in the Classroom   55

Use of Learning Principles   62

Types of Classroom Activities   69

Appropriateness of Learning Materials and Content   76

The Intended Curriculum and Classroom Practices   78

4 Curriculum Decision Making and Attitudes   **83**

Influences on the Curriculum   85

Attitudes Toward the Curriculum   91

Highlighting the Issues   97

5 The School and Classroom Contexts   **105**

Physical Context   107

Social Context   108

Power of the Implicit Curriculum   117

6   Teachers in the Elementary School   **124**

   Personal Characteristics and Professional Preparation   125
   Teachers' Impact on the Professional Milieu   135
   The Teacher as Professional Educator   142

7   Satisfactory and Unsatisfactory Classrooms   **146**

   Rationale and Methodology   147
   Aspects of Classroom Life for Early Elementary Students   150
   Aspects of Classroom Life for Upper Elementary Students   156
   Toward a Definition of Satisfactory Classrooms   166

8   A Look to the Future   **171**

   Guidelines for Curriculum Reform   172
   Conclusion   176

Appendix   A Study of Schooling: General Description   **179**

   The Elementary School Sample   180
   Research Instruments   180

   References   183
   Index   187
   About the Author   192

Foreword

Most of the time, our system of schooling is not a subject of intense state and national concern. Satisfaction is largely a personal matter, focused on the school one's child attends. It is difficult to arouse public interest as, increasingly, parents with children in school are a minority group. They, too, tend to lose interest when their children are no longer there.

Perhaps, then, it is necessary to sound the alarm periodically if citizens without school-age children are to be reminded of the need for good schools. Such was the case following the launching of Sputnik in 1957 and, more recently, with publication of *A Nation at Risk* in 1983. In each case, the quality of our schools was portrayed as being closely related to the nation's safety and welfare. In the 5 years following the appearance of *A Nation at Risk*, hundreds of bills designed to tighten rules governing schools and teacher education have been passed by legislatures in most states. Yet, during these 5 years, there has been considerable disagreement among observers of the educational scene as to whether or not schools have improved. Some say that the shortcomings reported in research-oriented reports such as Boyer (1983) and Sizer (1984) have not been corrected and, indeed, are growing more serious. Few are willing to say that the schools have improved more than a little. A view becoming increasingly widespread as the decade of the 1980s grows to a close is that principals and teachers at the level of individual schools have not been adequately involved. There is talk of a "second wave" of reform designed to impact more directly on classrooms, which the top-down initiatives appear not to have reached.

The history of the 1980s appears to be repeating the history of the 1960s, when widespread changes in schools were presumed to be taking place. But Frances Klein, along with myself and several colleagues, concluded in 1970 that these changes were either nonevents or cosmetic rather than fundamental (Goodlad, Klein, & associates, 1974). More than a dozen years later, I reported the findings of a comprehensive study of a representative sample of schools, concluding that almost every aspect of schooling required reconstruction (Goodlad, 1984). That reconstruction has not occurred, whatever the rhetoric of improvement; consequently, our findings are as valid and commanding today as they were in 1984.

In this book, Dr. Klein reminds us of these findings with respect to the elementary schools of our sample. The agenda emerging is central: Among many reforms, we need a curriculum more congruent with agreed-upon district and state educational goals, instructional proce- dures designed to get every child meaningfully involved in learning, and radically different grouping procedures. Although this is an agenda to be addressed throughout the ecology of the entire educational system, its fulfillment rests, in the final analysis, with principals and teachers in individual schools.

We now have a substantial body of literature regarding the limita- tions of legislating reform in these areas (Wise, 1979), of trying to mas- termind from afar what will work best (House, 1974), and of trying to impose changes on the culture of the school (Sarason, 1982). Although the reports of lighthouse schools creatively improved by school faculties are compelling, the results of trying to disseminate these improvements widely are not encouraging.

Frances Klein is one of a growing number of educators who believe that the individual school is the center of successful educational change (Sirotnik, 1987). It responds slowly and often defensively, however, when it becomes the target of change. The response is much more positive and productive when a faculty itself engages in renewing its school in a context of support and encouragement.

This last statement may appear obvious, but it has escaped the attention and understanding of large numbers of people who would improve the schools. Even many principals and teachers don't readily heed its meaning. There are at least two reasons for this: First, they are accustomed to being told what to do and, second, they have had very little experience with self-directed school renewal. Told that they are free to take the initiative, principals and teachers often do not know where or how to begin.

Frances Klein, herself a former elementary school teacher who, along with her colleagues, took advantage of the opportunity to be creative when it was offered, understands both the limitations of inno- vations imposed on schools and the encouragement teachers need to undertake significant change on the inside. Thus, as this book attests, her approach to individual school renewal is empathic and highly practical.

   Although her book has much to offer anyone interested in school improvement, her intended audience, clearly, is those adults who work each day in schools. To this audience she presents at least four very important areas of concern. First, she sees schools and those who work in them as being part of a large and important enterprise much in need of refurbishment. She uses extensive data to support an agenda of reform for schools generally. Second, she paints a picture of how schools would look if they performed more ideally. Third, she argues effectively for a process of change driven by those responsible for each individual school. And, fourth, she identifies a practical beginning point: knowledge of what is strongest and weakest within the context of a given school, knowledge readily accessible to and obtainable by each faculty group.

   The efforts of faculty, by themselves, will not be sufficient. The support and participation of parents, the district, and the state are essential. Even if those inside and outside of schools pull together, the task of getting the schools we need will be difficult. Without such collaboration, it will be impossible.

John I. Goodlad
May 1988

Preface

This book is intended as a resource for educators who would like to engage in curriculum reform as a reflective, deliberate, and informed process at the local level. It presents a possible way for a school faculty to examine its own programs and values before embarking on a course of curriculum reform. It does not offer a quick or easy path to reform; rather, it suggests possible ways of working with faculty members who care about the quality of the educational program and who want to continue what is already being done well, improve what needs to be strengthened, and introduce what may be missing from the program. It will assist administrators and teachers in being reflective about the school and in planning for change based upon the school's own agenda, not the platform of other educational reformers.

More specifically, this book raises questions and supplies some possible answers about fundamental elements of curriculum that are always involved in reform efforts. Tinkering with only one part of a school or curriculum will not produce meaningful change. The school as an institution must be broadly considered in any reform effort. Therefore, the elements addressed in this book are curriculum, teachers, students, and school and classroom practices. This book will show how a school can plan and collect data about these elements in schooling and use the data as a basis for understanding what the school is currently doing. This process is a necessary basis for informed and lasting change. It encourages faculty and administrators to think about whether or not they like what is occurring in their school and which aspects they may want to change.

This book, then, is an attempt to help *you* — an interested educator at the local school level — to take charge of how you will reform or improve your curriculum. It should be a resource to you in three different ways. First, it presents some research data from A Study of Schooling, which was a survey of a national sample of schools. These data provide a basis of comparison for the data you collect at your school (Goodlad, 1984), allowing you to see your school in relation to a national sample. Second, the discussions in the various chapters illustrate a process for summarizing and interpreting your data, a process that you can follow as you study your school and formulate a plan for curriculum improvement. Third, the discussion of the data from A Study of Schooling identifies specific elements that you can use in constructing the research instruments that will best enable you to examine similar aspects of your school closely and systematically.

Without a knowledge of what your school is like and how your faculty would like it to change, it is impossible to develop a deliberate, informed program for curriculum improvement. Without an examination of the issues and implications related to the changes proposed for curriculum improvement, changes may well occur simply for the sake of change — and they may well create new and unanticipated problems. Merely buying into someone else's reform proposal is to become subjected to someone else's ideas. This book, then, should be a resource for you in developing your own program of curriculum improvement.

ROLE OF RESEARCH DATA IN THIS BOOK

The data included in this book are heavily skewed toward curriculum and instruction. These are the substance of schooling and ought to be the central focus for any educational reform. Any other improvements must be designed to *support* the desired curriculum and modes of instruction; thus, they run the risk of being misdirected if attempted first. At the same time, however, it is recognized that all influences on the school — parents, administrators, teachers, students, the contexts of schooling, and interactions between teachers and students — potentially affect curriculum and instruction. Data on these important elements of schooling are also included, but they are discussed primarily in relation to the two fundamental concerns.

The amount of research data reported on in this book is extensive. The questions raised and the answers suggested in each chapter present a model your school faculty might follow in developing a school-based improvement plan. Reform activity ought to be a continuous process and not initiated only in response to the latest attempts at curriculum change. The questions raised are based upon research data from the sample of elementary schools in A Study of Schooling (Goodlad, 1984). (See the Appendix for a summary of the research sample and procedures used in A Study of Schooling.) The value of these data, however, is not inherent; it will be determined by how your school faculty decides to use them.

It is not necessary for you to be concerned about all aspects report-ed here at any one time. The importance of the data is that they repre-sent essential aspects of schooling related to curriculum and instruction, and any of these aspects is a potential starting place for your faculty to begin reflecting upon what kind of a school you have and what you would like it to become. Any area could be the launch point for your efforts to explore how similar your school is to the schools in the research sample, to construct your own items and instruments in order to collect your own data and organize them into meaningful segments, and to explore what the data mean for your own school. It is not my intention that you copy instrumentation used in A Study of Schooling. For one thing, the research instruments for studying your own school will not need to be as complex or as extensive as ours.[1] You will want to choose only those segments of data that represent your most immediate inter-ests and concerns about your school. Those that are not currently rele-vant may be skipped over, to be returned to later if needed. Changes will occur slowly and deliberately, and they can begin in any number of places. Ultimately, however, any change must be viewed in relation to all the important aspects of schooling.

The value of the extensive research data in this book is to remind your faculty that the job is not done by examining only one part of the school or curriculum. You must persist until all aspects have been stud-ied. By then, the change process should be a familiar one that can be engaged in on a continuous, nonthreatening basis. Only then will your school meet the challenge of providing the kind of education needed for your students.

Since this is not strictly a research report, the statistical analysis and explanation of the research data are not given in great detail. Those who desire more extensive documentation of the data on which the discussions in this book are based may refer to the original reports of the study. These are cited throughout this book.

In the long run, the basis for improving your curriculum should be the pursuit of adequate answers to such questions as, What is my school like? How would I like it to be? How can I help close the gap? Enlight-

---

[1]Information about the instruments used in A Study of Schooling is available from me. You can write me at the Department of Curriculum and Instruction, University of Southern California, Los Angeles, CA 90089-0031. Please be specific about which instru-ment you are interested in.

ened answers to these questions, reached through a careful, deliberate, and rational process, will insure that your elementary school classrooms will meet the demands of curriculum reform, thus assisting your students in effectively taking their places as prepared members of our complex, ever-changing society.

Finally, there are many people to whom I owe a debt of gratitude for helping this book come to fruition. I would like to acknowledge here those who had the greatest impact.

To my curriculum professors, who are now my friends and who have greatly influenced my thinking and work in the field of curriculum:

> John I. Goodlad, for helping me as a young, beginning teacher and introducing me to the study of curriculum; for encouraging me to continue my studies over many years; and for providing opportunities for many varied experiences in curriculum research and practice
>
> Louise L. Tyler, for teaching me to inquire into the field of curriculum and to appreciate diverse viewpoints

To my colleagues at the Institute for Development of Educational Activities (I/D/E/A), for their willingness and openness in sharing research reports and interpretations of data—their importance is documented throughout this book.

To my family, for all their support:

> My husband, Bill, for encouraging me in so many ways during the writing and rewriting of this book, for carrying more than his fair share of home responsibilities over the past few months, and for his infinite patience in teaching me word-processing skills so this book could become a reality
>
> My children, Karen and Steven, for all the time they allowed me to devote to the writing of the book
>
> My parents, for enabling me to take advantage of the opportunities that came my way

CURRICULUM REFORM
in the
ELEMENTARY SCHOOL

Creating Your Own Agenda

CHAPTER 1

Overview: Process and Substance of Curriculum Reform

Curriculum reform is once again being mandated by powerful forces and groups in our society. Blue-ribbon commissions (e.g., Adler, 1982; National Commission on Excellence in Education, 1983) and prestigious research reports (e.g., Boyer, 1983; Goodlad, 1984) have highlighted the need for reform and proposed standards and recommendations for guiding school faculties in achieving the recommended changes. Higher standards, more time on task, stronger academic courses, an extended school day and year, more homework, and revised teacher preparation are among the proposals being made by these very influential studies, reports, and groups.

The picture of our schools reflected in these calls for reform ranges from mediocre to good, but always in need of significant improvement. Although there is much agreement on the changes being proposed, as just listed, there is enough debate about them to suggest that perhaps they should not be implemented wholesale without a closer examination of what they mean for our schools, teachers, students, and society. What do they mean particularly for those who are most directly involved in curriculum reform — the administrators, teachers, and students? Are the current practices in the schools so lacking that the proposed reforms will be difficult to put into place, or are some of the recommended reforms already reflective of current practice? How can a school faculty determine whether or not they support the reform efforts? If they do not, how can an alternative set of standards be formulated for school improvement? These are essential questions that schools must address before meaningful and lasting curriculum reform can occur. They are also the questions that will be addressed in this book. The intent of this book is to help you — the educator serious about curriculum reform — determine your own program of curriculum improvement, based on research data.

Curriculum reform is not a new topic in the United States. The urgency for improving our schools seems to occur in almost predictable cycles. Even the newest desired reforms have a familiar ring to those of us who have been educators for awhile. The details may change over time, but the fundamental aspects of some past school reform efforts seem to be similar to the current ones. The schools are not perceived as providing our children with the kind of education needed for the changing times. Reforms, thus, center upon how to update schooling and better prepare our students for coping with a rapidly changing world, in accordance with the latest opinions about what needs to be done.

One major attempt to reform the curriculum, some will recall, occurred during the 1960s and was especially fueled by the Soviet launching of Sputnik. In fact, it was called the "curriculum reform era," and recommendations were made for such changes as expansion of the curriculum to include more academic subject areas, more rigorous and up-to-date content, improved teaching methods, more challenging activities for students, inquiry into subjects rather than mastery of a body of static knowledge, better use of classroom time, and greater achievement by students (Goodlad, Von Stoephasius, & Klein, 1966). As can be seen, the ideas of the 1960s are not entirely foreign to the current round of cries for reform.

Few oppose such changes, since they represent fundamental ways our schools are expected to prepare students as educated citizens. Surely, many say, the needed changes represent standards for reform that we can legitimately ask of our schools. Indeed, the reform movement of today has generated extensive support, both among professional educators and the lay public.

Why, then, are there repetitive cycles of educational reform? Why is it necessary to have periodic calls for renewed efforts to improve curricula? In part, it is because the research evidence regarding schools' past response to calls for reform documents a surprisingly stubborn resistance to the changes and a strong persistence in "business as usual" (e.g., Goodlad, Klein, & associates, 1974). Somehow our schools continue their traditional practices, in spite of powerful calls for reform and attempts to change practice. Something, clearly, is amiss in attempts at curriculum reform.

There exists an impressive body of research on how educational change occurs, documenting the necessary conditions for lasting change, the need for local school support as faculties attempt to change, the importance of the local school in school improvement, and the impact of different origins of change (e.g., Goodlad, 1975; McLaughlin & Marsh, 1978; Tye & Novotney, 1975). Impressive though this research is, much of it seems to be ignored when calls for reform go out across the nation. For example, research suggests that change is typically viewed by educators, not as a set of standards that must be set in place, but as a process that must directly involve those most affected by change. This requires extensive local school support for the process; it does not require the overseeing of static changes being put in place by subordinates. Pronouncements from governmental agencies or prestigious citizen groups will not necessarily be enthusiastically accepted by teachers and administrators. Without commitments and considerable effort directed toward change by the local school faculty, desired changes from on high do not seem to be implemented behind the classroom door (Goodlad et al., 1974).

REFORM AT THE LOCAL LEVEL

What should be the role of a school faculty in responding to these recurrent demands for curriculum reform? How can your faculty get involved in the process of change so that the reforms called for will really be addressed — and implemented, if they are what you want? How do you determine whether the reforms are appropriate for and needed at your school? Many school faculties have simply accepted the currently proposed standards and are hard at work trying to reform their programs to meet them, without much consideration of why they have adopted them or of their impact on teachers, students, and the broader society. These schools are often heralded as forward-looking and energetic, dynamic models for others to follow. If only all school faculties would be so diligent, our schools would, indeed, be successful at last — or so some reformers believe.

To the contrary, I believe that no school should just "jump on the bandwagon" of any current program of reform. Lasting and meaningful change is best assured when faculty determine what their current practices are and how their school should change, if at all. This requires a deliberate, studied approach. This, then, is the primary recommendation of this book: Study your own school and adopt a curriculum improvement plan that is specifically developed for your school with your faculty.

The current calls for reform come from very prestigious groups and individuals. Their rhetoric, and sometimes their research data, are very persuasive of the need for reform and of their standards as the ones to be used to guide it. Clearly, some carefully thought out proposals have been made, sound documentation of the need for change has been presented, and impressive plans for advancing the changes have been formulated. Who can quarrel with higher standards, more time in school, and higher achievement? These would seem to be the perennial "stuff" of excellence in education for our nation. What could be wrong with adopting them and getting on with the improvement of your curriculum?

Upon reflection, educators have given good reasons to be cautious in the wholesale adoption of curriculum reform proposals. They have observed that the current reform efforts all originate from the top; that is, they have been proposed by people who are beyond the local school level, although in very prestigious educational and societal positions. Proposals for reforms from these sources, however, do not have a very good history of lasting in the tradition-bound culture of our schools. Reforms have been diminished or lost at the classroom door in the past (Goodlad et al., 1974) because the conditions necessary for change have not been present. This suggests one reason for not adopting someone else's proposal for your school: It may not be implemented if mandated by groups beyond the local school.

Some educators have further observed that any proposed reform has a cost that must be examined carefully. When one part of the curriculum is changed, other parts are necessarily affected and must be reexamined. Changes must be looked at particularly for their impact on students. As Goodlad et al. (1966) noted during the 1960s push for school reform, studying a rigorous and demanding curriculum in a new subject area is not necessarily what a 6-year-old *ought* to be doing in the first grade. A comparable question is being raised now. Are higher achievement scores in reading and math worth the neglect of other highly desired goals of the curriculum, such as appreciation for the diversity in our culture, critical thinking, learning how to learn, and development of good citizenship skills (Goodlad, 1984; Klein, 1986)? These are the kinds of questions your school faculty ought to explore, and which this book will help you answer for your school.

A few of the leaders in the call for reform offer impressive documentation of what current practices are like in our schools and who they believe must deal with the proposals for reform. Others, however, offer pronouncements for reform with little or no support. Without understanding what a school faculty believes in and what it values in its educational program, meaningful change cannot occur. In addition, the faculty itself must see and accept the need for change.

The change process will need help from a variety of sources. It will require time for your faculty to engage in discussions, self-reflection, and the collection of data about important aspects of the current school program. It will require all of those in your school who want change and are expected to implement it to work beyond the regular hours of the classroom and school day. It will demand the use of scarce school resources. You will need the understanding and support of state, district, and local personnel, as well as the local lay community, as your faculty engages in reform efforts aimed at providing the quality of educational experience that you want for your students. Change is not easy, but it does characterize all good and effective schools.

ORGANIZING FOR CHANGE

A very important part of improving your curriculum is knowledge of the change process. Awareness of this will increase the probability of getting into practice the improvements the faculty decides upon as they deliberate on what their school is like and what they would like it to be. Each chapter of this book addresses some possible data-collection procedures and substantive changes you might want to build into your improvement plan, but it is up to you to formulate an effective procedural plan for bringing about the desired changes in your school. To do this, you will need to understand the substance and process of change. This section gives some general ideas about these two aspects.

Substance of Change

There are five substantive principles of change for you to remember as you develop your curriculum improvement plan.

Establishment of Central Goals. The primary focus of the plan is a critical factor. Your plan must emphasize what changes you would like to make, based on data collected about your school and a vision of what you would like it to be. Since curriculum is the foundation of schooling, your improvement plan should be primarily concerned with it. Any other reforms you may include, such as reorganization of the school or new procedures for selecting personnel, must be made in light of the curriculum changes you want.

Although all the details of the path to be traveled in the process of reform may not be known fully at the outset, the general destination should be agreed upon by most of your faculty members. Unless they hold some notion of what good education is and what desirable classroom practices are, change may only represent change for its own sake—that is, not change for the purpose of making something better, but just in order to do something different. The changes you make ought to be done in very specific ways for very good reasons.

Faculty discussion of what kind of change is needed and why it is desired is an important step in developing the substantive plan for change. Through these discussions and other means such as working with consultants and visiting other schools, your teachers will clarify what their values are regarding schooling and how these values should be reflected in the daily operation of their classroom. Your teachers may well resist these discussions by calling them useless philosophical speculation. Do everything you can to help them understand that philosophical discussions are not idle talk; they are fundamental to the change process. Without them, change may well be rudderless and aimless. A vision of good educational practice is essential to planned change. Change propelled by such a vision is likely to become a way of life for your school and teachers, rather than be rejected as too threatening an event or permitted as a one-time process to be avoided at all costs in the future.

Comprehensive Examination of Curriculum. The curriculum must be comprehensively defined and examined from all aspects. Any changes you expect to make should relate to a broad definition of all that you expect your school to do for your students. Avoid becoming engaged with only one or two narrow but fundamental aspects, such as reading and math. All the functions of schooling and all the goals of the curriculum you value must receive consideration as you make specific decisions regarding reform. Do not lose sight of the broad picture.

Analysis of Gap Between Theory and Practice. Although schools seem to be comfortable places for most students, there is room for much improvement. For example, our data suggested that the schools in our sample were not harming students in any significant way, but that there was much more that the schools could have been doing to improve the education of students. There was a serious gap between what the schools were expected to do and what they were actually doing. Any school can improve, no matter how good it might be. The emphasis on your curriculum improvement plan should be on closing the gap between actual practice and the vision of what is desired. Your school — any school — will always have such a gap. As practice improves, the vision can be revised to become even better. The message of this book is that you must determine where the gap exists at your school and work to close it. It may or may not be similar to other schools. It is essential that any plan for reform be *your* plan for improvement, designed specifically to fit your needs and desires.

Attention to Implicit Curriculum. In developing your substantive plan, pay close attention to the implicit curriculum — what we teach because we live in a social institution called a school — as well as the explicit curriculum — what we carefully and deliberately plan to teach. Students learn from both curricula, and so each must be monitored as closely as possible. We can no longer ignore or minimize the importance and impact of the implicit curriculum, as we have in the past. The potential messages it may convey to students are too important and too long lasting to overlook any longer (see chapter 5 for a more extensive discussion). Your curriculum plan must include a study of what the implicit curriculum is, and the attention given to it should be considered just as important as that given to the explicit curriculum.

Development of Systemic Approach. Any approach to curriculum improvement must be a systemic approach. One aspect of curriculum reform will have an impact on the other aspects of schooling. Taking a simplistic approach to change by considering only one aspect and expecting all else to continue as before is not realistic. The interrelationships among the various aspects of schooling must be recognized and provided for in your comprehensive plan for change. Curriculum, in particular, has a pervasive effect throughout the school. All aspects of change must be considered in relation first to the curriculum and then to other dimensions of the school. Even though you may focus on a particular part for a considerable length of time as the various aspects of the improvement plan are studied and implemented, ultimately you must focus on the systemic nature of school reform. Changes in one aspect of schooling must always be considered in relation to all other dimensions.

Process of Change

The specifics of the changes desired must be accompanied by some planning of the change process itself. Changes should occur as the result of a deliberately planned process, not haphazardly. The following recommendations for change have been abstracted from an impressive body of research on how the change process occurs. This discussion is not intended as a comprehensive review of that literature. (For further reading, see, for example, Fullan, 1982; Goodlad, 1975; McLaughlin & Marsh, 1978; Tye & Novotney, 1975.) What follows are four general recommendations about the change process which you should consider very carefully. They represent the second important part of your comprehensive plan for curriculum improvement.

Involvement of All Affected Parties. Change must involve those who live and work in the school and classrooms. Unless administrators, teachers, and students at the local school make an investment in the changes proposed, real change in the sense of lasting improvements that are incorporated into the ongoing life of the school or classroom will not be accomplished. People within the school must be committed participants in any change effort.

Emphasis on Action Research. Curriculum change should be considered to be an inquiry process. It is an investigation into what your school is actually like, not how you assume your school or classrooms to be. This suggests an important role for an analysis of research in general, but, more specifically, for conducting action research. A review of research in general — of studies such as those reported in this book — can identify problems that some schools have grappled with and suggest some possible solutions. It also can describe good procedures and recommendations for conducting a study of your school. It will not help, however, to identify specific local issues and problems being confronted by your school faculty. Action research at the local level is needed for that.

Action research refers to studies that are conducted at the grassroots level, not necessarily by professional researchers, but nonetheless following good research principles and procedures. It is carefully designed to identify and resolve the specific problems and difficulties of a particular school, teacher, or classroom and to inquire into the conditions of schooling (e.g., Klein, 1983; Longstreet, 1982). The principles of action research will help you in thinking about change as a process of inquiry into what schooling ought to be and what your school is like.

Assessment of Helpers and Hindrances. A careful study must be made of potential local barriers and facilitators to the change process. People or conditions that will hinder the process of getting into place the changes that you want must be identified and addressed in a deliberate and forthright manner, not ignored or mishandled. This will require good communication skills, an honest and inquiring approach to change, and the courage to stand behind and defend your convictions. Try not to be caught off guard by problems that could have been anticipated in advance and perhaps avoided, or at least made less debilitating by careful planning.

At the same time, identify all possible resources that will facilitate the change process. No potential aid should be overlooked, no matter how small. Sometimes just a sympathetic ear from one who understands is all that is needed to overcome a hurdle that is in the offing. Potential sources of ideas and funding that could help in making the changes you want should be identified. Ways should be formulated for recognizing the efforts of those who work hard in developing the plan and attain some degree of success in making the changes.

Establishment of a Broad Community Base. The process of change requires a broad base of communication and participation. Your school and its classrooms do not exist in isolation; they are always a part of a larger whole which must be considered. The identification and involvement of all the groups important in curriculum improvement must occur. Groups in the community, particularly your students' parents, must be involved in or at least be made knowledgeable about most school changes, as must many other publics who have a vested interest in what your school is like. Your district and county offices must be informed and involved to some degree, since your school is an essential part of those entities. Even when change occurs in one of your classrooms, it must be recognized that the classroom exists in relation to other classrooms. Discussions with other teachers need to be held, administrators kept informed, parents involved or at least informed, and students helped to understand how they will be affected. Schools are an important part of our democratic society and as such are responsible to a large number of different people and groups. Those with an interest in your school must not be forgotten as you engage in the process of change.

GETTING STARTED AND MAINTAINING MOMENTUM

In this section we are concerned with concrete steps to be taken in organizing for change and maintaining momentum once you have begun. Six recommendations are discussed which should help you get started and keep going in your plan for curriculum improvement.

Establishing a Core Group. The best way to develop energy for a project is to involve only those who really want to be involved initially. This group should be large enough to sustain dialogue and represent the school at various levels, if at all possible. The literature on change often refers to a "critical mass" of people being important to the process. For your elementary school this means you should have a small group initially, perhaps 5 to 10 people, who are successful, respected leaders in the school and competent practitioners. Do not attempt to involve anyone at first who is resistant to change and who is completely satisfied with what they are doing. Rather, try to involve those who are open to change, want to improve, and are eager to examine what they do in the classroom and why.

Developing a Vision. Devote time to discussions of what you would like your school to be like, what type of students you have and what type you hope your efforts are helping to develop, and what the overall goals and purposes are for your curriculum. You need to create for yourselves a vision of what you would like schooling to be like before you will know what and how to change.

The substance of the next six chapters of this book should help you get started in these discussions. Each addresses an important aspect of the curriculum itself or significant factors that affect the curriculum. These could be used as the basis for faculty meetings, grade-level group sessions, or after-school meetings of just those few teachers and administrators who are really interested in creating a vision for reform. As change begins to occur, perhaps these topics could be a focus for faculty meetings. Sharing your vision will help keep all the teachers at your school informed about, and perhaps ultimately get them involved in, the efforts toward curriculum improvement.

Choosing Topics for Discussion. Select one chapter of this book or even one section as a focus for your discussions. Choose the one that generates the most interest in the beginning discussions and is directly related to the ongoing work of the classroom. Do not feel compelled to conform to the research findings; rather, look upon those reports as sources of examples for how you may collect and organize your own data and make sense out of them. Using the research instruments from A Study of Schooling as guides, plan your own questions and instruments, collect your data, and summarize and analyze what your data mean. Then decide what, if anything, needs improvement and how to do it.

Organizing Meetings. Arrange a regular meeting time and place for continuing your work. Curriculum improvement will not occur with haphazard meetings and efforts. It will need sustained attention over time and the best efforts of your school's most outstanding leaders. Come prepared to meetings with ideas and data, and be ready to use them as a basis for action to improve the curriculum. Work on curriculum improvement needs prime time, not times when your teachers are weary and preoccupied. If at all possible, set the meeting times during the school day and arrange for substitutes or some other way of covering the classrooms. If release time from the classroom is not possible, meet whenever you can, under as pleasant circumstances as can be created. Perhaps the atmosphere and the excitement of really improving your school will overcome even the weariness at the end of a school day, should that be the only available meeting time.

Developing Short- and Long-Range Plans. Focus on what needs to be done by the next meeting or over the next few meetings, and be sure that everyone understands the tasks outlined. Also keep in mind where you ultimately want to go with your efforts and how gradually to involve more and more of your faculty. Eventually you will want to engage as many of your faculty as possible in your study group, but in ways that do not disrupt your progress. Plan how this can be done over the long term.

Keeping Things Moving. Do not be dismayed if all members of your faculty do not share your interest in and enthusiasm for school reform. Some teachers will not choose to be involved in this important process, for reasons of their own — some legitimate and others not. Persist in your efforts, regardless, and rely on the support of those who are most interested and who will really benefit from it. Few schools will be able to involve their total faculty, and even then the participation will be uneven. Encourage those who choose to participate, reward them with whatever is available to keep them involved, and celebrate your progress at intervals so that your sense of movement is apparent.

You will have to evolve a way of working together that is comfortable and productive for your own group. Do devote some attention to process as you continue your efforts, remembering that you are engaged in the most fundamental task of improving your school. Nothing could be more important.

SUMMARY

There is little doubt regarding the importance of the current interest in and perceived need for school improvement, but it is essential that reform not be undertaken on the basis of someone else's agenda. Curriculum improvement is an inquiring process that must be engaged in by members of your school faculty. That process should be based upon a knowledge of what your school is like and a vision of how you would like it to be. How to close any gaps you identify becomes the basis of your curriculum improvement program.

In order to engage effectively in reform efforts, you will need an understanding of the substance of change for any curriculum improvement program and of the process of change itself. You will need to know how to get organized and maintain momentum as you embark in your process of inquiry and develop your own curriculum improvement program. The support and involvement of those who are truly interested is crucial.

Through the process of deliberating about what your values are, defining your vision of what schooling ought to be, and collecting data about your own school, members of your faculty will set their own curriculum improvement agenda and will engage in the essential ongoing process of change. In so doing, they help assure that your students will receive the kind of education they need, which, after all, is the fundamental purpose of curriculum reform.

CHAPTER 2

The Intended Curriculum

Curriculum is the substance of schooling. It is composed of what you expect students to learn and what they actually do learn as a result of spending a major portion of their lives in school. It is the primary purpose for the existence of your school. As such, it is of basic importance in the improvement of schooling. Although reforms can also be directed toward other aspects of the school, such as the organizational structure, sources for funding, teacher and student roles, and administrative responsibilities, all of these are studied with the ultimate intent of improving the curriculum of the school.

This chapter discusses one aspect of the curriculum — the intended curriculum. This is what students are expected to learn; it is instruction that is deliberately and intentionally planned for the students. The intended curriculum is the result of the planning phase of the curriculum development cycle and reflects the hopes, aims, and expectations of many different people for what should happen for students during the time they spend in school. In this chapter we will discuss four specific sources from which the intended curriculum was derived in the schools we studied. These sources include: (1) perceptions of what the functions of schooling ought to be and actually were in the schools, (2) the content of curriculum guides, (3) the types of learning materials available and used, and (4) sources of potential influence over what teachers were expected to teach. These components of the intended curriculum can have a powerful influence over what your students learn in the elementary school and thus need careful attention by your faculty as you plan your program of curriculum improvement.

The term *curriculum* is used so frequently in any discussion of schooling that the lack of agreement about its meaning is usually masked, despite the fact that the disagreement is often extensive and of long standing. The lack of agreement is due to differing value positions or conceptions about what students should experience while they are in school and what type of person students should be when they are educated. (For summaries of these debates, see, for example, Eisner & Vallance, 1974; McNeil, 1985; Pinar, 1975.) The position you take regarding these important value debates will influence the curriculum in

13

your school. It will determine, for example, whether your curriculum will emphasize thinking skills, becoming a better person, developing a storehouse of fundamental knowledge and skills, creating a more just and equitable society, or some combination of these broad value positions (Eisner & Vallance, 1974; Klein, 1986). For you to achieve consensus on which of them ought to be the basis of your curriculum is not an easy task. It is, however, a fundamental one which must be addressed when improvements for your school are charted.

Although your faculty may be prone to dismissing such discussions as meaningless and not practical, it is essential that a clear vision be developed as to what schools should do for and with students. The vision you develop about what your curriculum should be will play an important role in the clarification of the intended curriculum, and it will require that you answer some basic questions, such as the following:

- What are the basic functions and goals of your curriculum?
- What should be taught?
- What materials are available and used?
- Do the materials support the kind of curriculum you want?
- What are the sources of influence on what your teachers teach and how successful are they?

As you read in this book the discussions of the data from A Study of Schooling, you are encouraged to speculate about how your school might respond to these and other questions. Even though the data reported are not generalizable to all schools, the questions being discussed are. It is also hoped that you will develop your own instruments, in order to collect comparable data about the components of the intended curriculum for your school, and then use that data as one basis for curriculum improvement.

SURVEYING THE EDUCATIVE FUNCTIONS OF SCHOOLING

One of the most fundamental questions that can be asked regarding curriculum is, What should be taught? Your answer to this question will help determine what your students have an opportunity to learn, and this clearly will have a tremendous impact on the lives of your students, while they are in school and well after they leave school. What subjects will be included in the curriculum? How will the content be organized? What problems, concepts, skills, or processes should be taught? Your faculty is responsible for how these questions are responded to, whether it is done as a result of overt deliberation or as a result of simply accepting the way things have always been done. Since the issue is such a fundamentally important one, it deserves to be addressed through comprehensive, enlightened deliberation and not be left to chance or tradition or be put in outsiders' hands.

It must be recognized, of course, that the question of what should be taught is different from what is actually taught. It is normally assumed that the answer to the latter question flows from the answer to the former, with some interaction between the two. And yet, that assumption may not be warranted in some cases, perhaps in most cases. In many schools a great deal of effort is expended in answering the question as to what should be taught, through the use of surveys of parents, the identification of state mandates, discussions with community leaders, the use of state curriculum guides, the preparation of district curriculum guides, the selection of learning materials, and the use of consultants. Equal attention, however, is not given to helping teachers translate these expectations into reality — into what is actually taught. But for now, that is a question to be set aside and answered in the next chapter. The focus here is upon what is expected to be taught — the intended curriculum.

In A Study of Schooling, a variety of data were obtained which helped answer the question of what should be taught, and our data could be an important impetus as you begin your study of the intended curriculum. The data included a series of questions asked of parents, teachers, and students regarding which of four educative functions they believed were important and which one of these should be and actually was emphasized at their particular school. An extensive analysis of state and district guides was conducted, some aspects of which were directly related to the question of what the intended curriculum should be. Also, an analysis of curriculum materials submitted by teachers helped to support the answer to the question. Finally, our teachers were asked about 11 potential sources of influence on what they were expected to teach. All of these data help to formulate an answer to the question of what the intended curriculum was for this sample of schools.

It is generally agreed that, although schools serve diverse functions such as socializing students into the dominant culture and providing custodial care, they exist primarily for the educative function. Within this educative function, however, it is possible to have varying emphases. We selected four major ones for study: intellectual, social, personal, and vocational development of students. These four educational emphases represent a broad range of possible goals for the intended curriculum of your school. For example, if your school emphasizes intellectual development, it would stress achievement in the basic skills of mathematics, reading, writing, and verbal communication, and of critical thinking and problem solving. If your school chooses to emphasize the social development of your students, you would be most concerned about preparing them to get along with other students, preparing them for social and civic responsibilities, and developing their awareness and appreciation of their own and other cultures. If the personal development of students is emphasized, building self-confidence, developing creativity, thinking independently, and fostering self-discipline would be stressed. Finally, with an emphasis on vocational development, you would try to prepare students for employment, develop the necessary skills for getting a job, and develop awareness about career choices and alternatives. These are the most common educative emphases and would determine, to some degree at least, what should be taught in your intended curriculum.

A major task for your school faculty is to determine which areas of development are considered important by the people most concerned about your school. It is likely that several would be chosen to guide the intended curriculum. In fact, most schools would find it difficult to reject any of these outright but would be able to prioritize their relative importance to the curriculum.

It would be much simpler in the process of studying your school if all groups involved (teachers, students, parents, and administrators) gave corroborating responses to questions relating to the school's educative functions. This is not likely to be the case, of course, so you will need to ask the same questions of all the major groups and then compare their answers, looking for discrepancies and points of agreement.

To this end, we asked teachers and parents to indicate for each of the four educational emphases how important they perceived it to be on a scale ranging from "very important" to "very unimportant." Since it was possible that what was *desired* by the different groups was not necessarily *practiced* at the school they know best, we asked them whether their school actually addressed each of those functions. Finally, we asked the groups to consider, if they had to choose only one emphasis out of the four, which one it would be, and which one they believed was actually being pursued the most at their school. Thus we asked for responses to four areas of inquiry:

1. The importance each emphasis actually had at the respondent's school
2. The importance each emphasis should have at the respondent's school

3. The single emphasis that actually was most pursued at the respondent's school
4. The single emphasis that ought to be most pursued at the respondent's school

Comparing the answers to these questions allowed the assessment of congruency of perception among the groups, with regard to their desires and actual practice.

Although these questions were asked of both teachers and parents, students at the upper elementary level (grades 4 through 6) were asked only the two to which we believed they could best respond: what they thought actually was the most important emphasis at their school, and what they thought should be the most important emphasis. Thus, they were asked to select only *one* emphasis rather than respond to all four. (Early elementary students were not asked any of these questions.)

As might be anticipated, both parents and teachers within the elementary sample replied that each of the four emphases of schooling was very important (Overman, 1980a). Further, they agreed that, of the four, developing the intellectual abilities was the single most important and that their particular school, indeed, emphasized that one. At this broad level, then, there was considerable congruence between the two groups regarding what ought to be and what was occurring at their school.

As noted, the upper elementary students were asked to select only the single most important function. Their responses were somewhat more varied, but still in agreement with the general perceptions of teachers and parents. At a more specific level of analysis, however, there were some interesting variations in the responses. A closer look at the responses to each area of inquiry is warranted.

Importance Each Emphasis Actually Had at Respondent's School

Over half of the teachers in the elementary school sample believed that intellectual, social, and personal development were considered important to the curriculum at their school (see Table 2.1). As might be expected, the vocational aspect was seen as less important for elementary schools, although almost one-fifth of the teachers said that it, too, was very important.

Parents of the elementary school sample tended to follow the same pattern as the teachers in their ratings of each emphasis at their school, although the scores for the first three were all somewhat lower than the teachers'; whereas their estimate of the importance of the vocational emphasis was a bit higher.

Table 2.1 Parents', Teachers', and Students' Perceptions of the
Relative Importance of Educational Emphases

Perception (% yes)	Educational Emphasis			
	Intellectual	Social	Personal	Vocational
Is very important				
Teachers	88.5	54.8	57.0	19.1
Parents	74.0	44.6	50.6	25.5
Should be very important				
Teachers	92.1	86.0	92.8	41.4
Parents	91.1	73.8	87.1	52.6
Is most emphasized				
Teachers	78.5	12.2	6.1	3.2
Parents	68.9	13.6	11.4	6.0
Students	61.4	11.1	11.9	15.5
Should be most emphasized				
Teachers	48.9	14.0	33.5	3.6
Parents	57.6	9.3	24.5	8.6
Students	47.1	13.8	17.3	21.8

Source: Overman, 1980a

Importance Each Emphasis Should Have
at Respondent's School

A similar but even stronger pattern of responses by teachers and
parents occurred when they were asked about the desirability of each
emphasis, that is, whether an emphasis on each function *should* be
present in their school (refer to Table 2.1). Well over three-fourths of the
teachers said each of the emphases, except for vocational, should be
important. Although sizable numbers of the teachers thought all the
emphases were desirable, clearly the vocational emphasis was perceived
as less desirable than the other three to a good number of teachers. This
pattern of responses was also reflected by the parents, who thought that
all the emphases *should* be important for their school, but saw the
vocational aspect as the least important of the four areas. As in the
previous case of ratings of how important each area actually *was* at their
school, the parents' percentages were lower than the teachers' for intellectual, social, and personal but higher for vocational.

There clearly was some support, then, for the curriculum to have
multiple thrusts in terms of what should be taught in this sample of
schools. A curriculum with a singular thrust on intellectual development might well have been judged as inadequate by large numbers of

our teachers and parents, as they also showed high regard for social and personal development and considered vocational development to be of some importance as well. Further, there was a considerable degree of congruence between how teachers and parents believed these emphases ought to exist and how they were perceived to exist in practice at their particular school. This suggests that there should have been considerable satisfaction about the curriculum — and we will see later from other data that this was true.

The Single Emphasis That Actually Was Most Pursued at Respondent's School

Another part of the series of questions about the functions of schooling asked teachers, students, and parents to select the one area of development they thought *was* most pursued at their school. When forced to select only one of the four, all three groups clearly selected the intellectual emphasis (see Table 2.1). Each of the other emphases received less than 20% of the responses. This would certainly be expected, given the high level of support accorded to the intellectual area in the preceding questions. Any major deviation from what is desired and what is actually emphasized at your school could be a source of considerable dissatisfaction. The data for this sample indicate overwhelming support for emphasis on the intellectual area of development, both in theory and in practice.

The Single Emphasis That Ought to Be Most Pursued at Respondent's School

Although the intellectual emphasis also was most often chosen by all three groups as the one that *ought* to be stressed, each of the other three areas received significant support (over 20%) from at least one of the three groups. The intellectual emphasis was preferred by the largest percentages of all three groups over the other three functions, yet it was chosen by only slightly less than half of the teachers and students, and slightly over half of the parents (see Table 2.1). In these days of "back to the basics" and stress placed upon higher cognitive processes (a major part of intellectual development), it was surprising that higher percentages of all three groups did not select the intellectual emphasis as *the* desired one. It seems clear that, for this elementary school sample, more was expected of the curriculum than the "back to the basics" leaders have advocated.

After the intellectual emphasis, personal development received the most support for being the one that ought to receive priority. It is interesting to note that fewer students at the elementary level rated the personal emphasis as being the one that ought to be stressed than did the other two groups, even though students' perception of actual emphasis on the personal area was close to that of the others. This discrepancy raises a number of interesting questions:

- Do students at this age level simply expect to do what adults ask of them at school, or do they expect their personal development to occur outside school rather than within school?
- Is their vision of schooling such that they expect that the school ought only to help them develop intellectually and not in other ways?
- How do some of the students think the school is helping them in personal development?

Similarly, other discrepancies indicate important trends in the data. Only about half of the teachers thought the intellectual emphasis was the one that should be most stressed, but over three-fourths believed it was the one most pursued at their school. At the same time, a third of the teachers thought the personal emphasis should be the one most pursued, but less than 10% thought it was the one most pursued. Clearly, there was support for adding more goals to the curriculum reflecting the personal development of students — perhaps even at the expense of less time being spent on intellectual goals.

Parents were in more general agreement about what was and what ought to be pursued at their schools than were teachers and students. Even so, about a quarter of the parents thought the personal emphasis ought to be the one most pursued, while only slightly over 10% thought it was. Again, there was support for adding greater emphasis to personal goals in the curriculum.

Would parents and teachers be supportive of more time spent on goals in the personal domain even if it meant less time spent on intellectual development? What types of personal goals would they support? These are important and interesting questions for your faculty to ponder and study further, if you discover comparable perceptions at your school.

Greater congruence was expressed for the social emphasis, although the number within each of the three groups selecting this as the preferred emphasis was small. The numbers of teachers and parents who preferred the vocational emphasis were also small, but more than a

fifth of the students in the upper grades of the elementary sample selected it. It also should be noted that vocational emphasis was second only
to intellectual emphasis for these students, and they differ from parents
and teachers in this respect. Why did so many students at this age level
prefer a vocational emphasis in the curriculum? Perhaps the need for
schooling in order to get a good job had been sold well to the children,
perhaps even too well. Although the vocational emphasis usually received less support than the other three, across all four areas of inquiry,
the percentages in many cases were large enough to warrant careful
consideration by your faculty, should you find comparable results. The
vocational function may need to be a part of your intended curriculum
if it is supported by enough parents, teachers, and students.

The Need to Keep an Open Mind

You may be tempted to assume that, because you have a particular
type of student body, you know what functions of schooling will be
desired by your groups. Our data suggest that you should not assume
this. For example, a common perception of many people is that the
schools in which minority students predominate would be more likely to
emphasize the vocational aspect; that parents of lower socioeconomic
status might perceive schooling as a way of helping their children get
better jobs. This perception, however, was not reflected in this sample of
schools. Three schools had all three groups (teachers 3–18%, students
20–30%, and parents 11–30%) showing some preference for a vocational
emphasis, but in only one of them did minority students — Mexican-
Americans — predominate. The other two schools had a mixed student
body. In one of these schools, which had a racially mixed student body
and was located in a rural-suburban community, all three groups had
sizable percentages (20–31%) reporting that the vocational emphasis
was, indeed, pursued at the school. This was the only school where the
larger preferences for a vocational emphasis matched the perceptions of
the larger number of teachers, students, and parents as to what was
actually occurring. In another predominantly Mexican-American urban
school, some students and parents showed a preference for the vocational emphasis, but the teachers did not. A different school — one with a
white, rural population — had some parents (20%) and teachers (25%)
who reported that a vocational emphasis existed, but it was not desired
by the higher percentages of teachers and parents. Thus, there was little
in this sample to support the stereotypical notion that a minority-group
elementary school should offer a curriculum that pursues a vocational

emphasis so that the students will be well prepared for jobs. Not only were there small percentages overall of teachers, students, and parents who desired this and actually perceived it to be true at their schools, when there was congruence among the groups of those who desired it and perceived it to be so, the schools were different demographically. Schools with large numbers of minority students could not be differentiated from the other schools.

Thus, you should not assume that, because you have a certain type of student population, your parents, students, or teachers will necessarily agree on a certain function for the curriculum. The task is to ask your groups what they believe and then to study what those preferences and perceptions mean for the curriculum of your school.

A preference for the intellectual emphasis is clear in relation to the other three possible emphases, not only in what this sample of parents, teachers, and students thought schools ought to be doing but also in what they perceived was actually being done. This is an indication that what they value is being attended to in the curriculum. The resulting healthy view of their schools is supported by other data, to be discussed later.

A Broad View of Curriculum

Although there is undoubtedly a high level of importance attached to the intellectual emphasis in the curriculum, the data in Table 2.1 indicate there would be support for a much broader curriculum than the one that has been narrowly defined as "back to the basics." Substantial numbers of parents, teachers, and students believed that personal, social, and vocational development were also important. If these functions are actually to provide some direction to the intended curriculum, something more than the subjects as they are traditionally defined must be provided.

There clearly would be a difference between a curriculum that helps students accept civic responsibilities, get along with others, and appreciate their own and other cultures and a curriculum that primarily emphasizes learning important facts, processes, and concepts and to read, write, and compute. A broadly defined experiential social studies curriculum would need to be prominently featured in a school program in order to help students achieve the former goals. Similarly, developing self-confidence, creativity, self-discipline, and the ability to think independently would require taking some risks, making choices, being extensively involved in the arts, and taking time to reflect upon what is being learned. These are characteristics not typical of a curriculum with a narrow focus upon the basic traditional subjects. While a focus on the traditional basics would be *part* of a curriculum that met the desires of our sample, it certainly would have to extend well beyond them.

It is important that you determine how those in your school view the curriculum — what the areas are that your parents, teachers, administrators, and students believe ought to be and are being emphasized at your school. If theory and practice are not in congruence, there is likely to be considerable dissatisfaction with what is occurring at your school. In such an event, it may be necessary to help the different groups understand what contribution each of the areas can make to a child's education. Only if they have this knowledge can they wisely select the ones they want emphasized. The areas that are agreed upon by your constituent groups have great significance for setting the goals of your intended curriculum and for interpreting other data to be discussed in later chapters.

As you obtain data for your school on the functions that teachers, parents, and students perceive to be the most important, there are some important questions you might want to address:

1. Are you satisfied with what the data say about your curriculum? Do the emphases reported reflect what you really want your curriculum to be? If not, you may need to educate your parents, teachers, and students about the importance of the other emphases they did not select.
2. Is there a congruence between the perceptions of what should be and what actually is being emphasized at your school? If there is not, what might be the possible causes of the discrepancies, and are there any courses of action you might take in order to correct them?
3. How do the goals of the various subject areas line up with the emphases that are preferred by your teachers, parents, and students? For example, are social goals really being addressed by what is being taught in the social studies curriculum, and, if so, how are they being taught? Or, does something more need to be added, such as student government, community projects, or more cooperative work, in order to help the students reach the social goals of the curriculum?

These are the kinds of questions your faculty could profitably address, based upon the data you collect about the functions of schooling. Those functions that are believed to be important should be reflected in every aspect of the intended curriculum and in school and classroom practices. If they are not, you have a very important area to explore for curriculum improvement.

ANALYSIS OF CURRICULUM GUIDES

Curriculum guides in many school districts are considered to be basic documents. Much time and effort are spent in the production of guides, both at the state and district level. They are commonly as much a part of schools as are teachers, students, texts, and desks. They are a fixture of schools. More important than their prevalence, however, is that they are often considered to be a formal statement of the intended curriculum. Analyzing your curriculum guides can tell you what the writers and supporters of the documents believe ought to be included in the curriculum. In this section we will look at what the curriculum guides for our sample of schools had to say about the fundamental curricular questions.

An extensive analysis was conducted of 269 guides, including 122 state guides and 147 district guides for all grade levels (Klein, 1980a). Since there were no recognizable differences among guides for the elementary school and for other levels, the following discussion is based on the total sample.

Among the functions these guides were expected to serve were to specify content, update trends, and provide ideas for objectives and classroom practice for teachers — all of which helped define what was expected to be taught. Although the collection analyzed cannot be considered a representative sample, some aspects were so highly consistent from guide to guide that we wondered if guides written for any other schools could dare to be different. The consistent way the basic elements of curriculum planning were handled gave strong directions as to what the curriculum of those schools was expected to be.

Goals and Objectives

One of the most commonly addressed curricular elements in the guides was goals and objectives — statements of what students were expected to learn. The goals and objectives within the 269 guides analyzed were reflective of the disciplines, that is, the traditional organization of the curriculum by subject area. Goals for science, math, spelling, literature, and social studies, for example, were overwhelmingly typical of the subject areas included. It was a rare occurrence to find a goal that reflected other than the subject-matter-based curriculum. Few attempts, for example, were present in the sample of guides to combine subjects into an interdisciplinary approach or to reflect a problem-solving approach. Rarer still was any attempt to organize the curriculum around problems or needs of the society or to address the social goals of the curriculum except through the organized content of the social studies program. Also virtually absent was any reflection of the individual needs and interests of the student as a basis for organizing the curriculum.

Many of the subject-matter goals were translated into behavioral objectives. The strong emphasis in the curriculum literature and in current practice upon behavioral objectives was reflected very clearly in the guides. Any controversy about their desirability and usefulness, although present in the research literature, was not acknowledged in these guides. Indeed, the desirability of behavioral objectives was clearly endorsed and never questioned. The quality and consistency of the objectives varied significantly from guide to guide. Some guides contained broad, complex behavioral objectives reflecting significant changes desired in the student which would take place over an extended period of time. Others defined simple behavioral objectives very precisely and in great detail. In their attempt to make objectives observable and measurable, the authors of some guides confused learning activities with behavioral objectives; that is, the so-called objectives described what students were to do in the classroom rather than the behavioral outcomes they were to achieve. Still other guides contained very specific sequential behaviors to be achieved by students in short periods of time.

In addition to being behavioristic in their orientation, the guides also were very cognitively oriented. There was a strong emphasis on the development of the intellectual abilities of the students. Although it was not unusual for a guide to have affective goals that were designed to help students develop attitudes, interests, values, and emotions, these were very rarely translated into behavioral objectives. The affective goals remained at an abstract level, and teachers were given virtually no help in translating them into classroom practices. Psychomotor goals and objectives were included in guides in those subject areas where they would be most expected: reading, art, music, physical education, and vocational education.

The dominance of intellectual goals is in keeping with the fact that parents, teachers, and students in our sample choose intellectual development as *the* most important function of schooling. What has been lost, however, was the desire of the parents, teachers, and students to have social, personal, and (to a lesser extent) vocational development included in the curriculum. The curriculum guides we analyzed neglected these other functions by their exclusive focus on traditional subject matter and by the absence of affective objectives.

If your curriculum guides are at all similar to those in our sample, a starting place for school improvement could be to revise the guides to reflect the full range of curriculum outcomes you desire and to give teachers the kind of help they might need in translating these mandates into classroom practices.

Content

Another curricular element commonly included in the guides was content. It, too, reflected the basic subject areas (i.e., subject matter design) and ranged from very specific definitions of songs or jump-rope jingles to be taught, to very broad concepts, topics, and generalizations. The broad approach was by far the most common used in the definition of content. Few guides defined content in terms of basic processes within the disciplines or in terms of critical thinking skills. Approaches to problem solving, for example, were not commonly included as content, nor were the fundamental problems facing humankind today. The guides usually spelled out clearly what students were expected to learn as concepts, ideas, and generalizations from a particular subject area. As noted already, rarely if ever was it acknowledged that the interests and abilities of students should be a deliberate consideration in deciding what content should be taught. Interest and motivation on the part of students to learn what was spelled out from traditional subject areas were apparently assumed to exist and were not explicitly addressed in most guides.

Evaluation

In spite of the emphasis upon evaluation of skill attainment and achievement testing in the schools today, the guides gave little help to teachers for dealing with evaluation as a curriculum element. Perhaps it was assumed by many of the writers that teachers had the necessary skills with which to develop procedures and instruments on their own or that achievement tests were readily available by which to assess the content and behaviors included in the guide. Neither assumption is a valid one, based upon the research evidence. The types of tests teachers commonly develop are often not good examples of how to evaluate student learning (even though their tests reflect the general approach to content as spelled out in the guides), nor do standardized achievement tests necessarily reflect particular emphases in the local curriculum.

The fact that the curricular task of evaluating the progress of students was so neglected in the guides is very significant. Given the current use of standardized achievement tests in defining what will be taught in the curriculum and in holding teachers accountable for their students' learning, this was a very serious omission. Teachers are given virtually no help in determining whether or not their students are learning what they are expected to learn. If your teachers attempt to teach what is set forth in the guide, and if that content is not matched by the achievement test selected by your district to use, the accountability attempt has an extremely serious flaw, one that is fundamentally unjust to both teachers and students.

The lack of attention to the evaluation of student learning is also a serious limitation in making sure that what is expected to be taught does get translated into what is actually taught. It is easy for teachers to assume that, if they teach the required content, students will, of course, learn it. Much of schooling, however, defies this common-sense idea. Evidence of some type is needed to indicate the progress students are making toward all the stated goals and objectives of the curriculum. Evaluation is a fundamental aspect of curriculum development and of determining what is expected to be taught. The omission of it from the curriculum guides in our sample was a serious oversight. Teachers need and deserve much help from many sources, including curriculum guides, in the evaluation of what students are expected to learn.

Individualization

Missing, too, was help to teachers in individualizing the curriculum for students. It could be expected that, given the rhetoric in the literature on the importance of individualization, the guides would have this as an important theme; yet 200 of the 269 guides had nothing on the topic. When individualization was mentioned, it was usually in the form of an exhortation to teachers to do it, but very little help was given on how to go about it. By implication, then, the curriculum as defined in the guides was intended for all students, regardless of differences in achievement, abilities, or interests.

Also by implication, the teacher was viewed as a user of curricula, not as a primary decision maker about curricula. Although many of the guides were written in the tone of being suggestions and not prescriptions for the teacher, little or no help was given in modifying or adapting the curriculum to different groups, let alone to different individuals. It was an extremely rare guide that addressed the process of curriculum development explicitly so that teachers would be helped in becoming skillful in those processes. Rather, the guides were written for teachers to use in lieu of developing or even adapting the curriculum for their own students.

Traditional Roles

The guides also reflected traditional roles for the teachers and students. Teachers were viewed as the possessors of knowledge and were expected to impart it to their students. Any honest approach to problem solving (i.e., where the solution was not already known by the teacher) was much too rare. That the teacher sometimes might be a learner along with the students was an unrecognized role in the guides. It seemed to be the assumption that, if the teacher did not know the content, the students would not learn it. This is a very heavy responsibility for any elementary schoolteacher. With the technological capabilities we now have for storing and making available knowledge as needed, this is an assumption that must be reexamined (and will be, later in this chapter and in chapter 5). It is now possible for students to learn much that the teacher does not know. It is generally acknowledged that the technological advances in computer-based instruction could redefine the content of the curriculum and the roles of students and teachers. The whole concept of computer-based education is an area where your faculty could begin examining some fundamental questions of what the curriculum should be, the role of the teacher in dispensing content and in fulfilling other functions of the curriculum, and how the computer could be used most effectively in redefining the traditional view of curriculum.

Conclusions

The curriculum guides analyzed from the Study of Schooling sample presented to teachers a very traditional concept of the intended curriculum. The contents of the guides were generally familiar ones to teachers with some expertise in the subject areas. The curricula reflected were very traditional, subject-based, and exclusively cognitive. The guides defined content in broad terms, stated behavioral objectives for teachers to follow which varied greatly in their quality, and gave no help in individualizing the curriculum or in evaluating student learning. They offered little help to a faculty interested in improving their curriculum beyond what is typically planned and offered, in order to better meet a variety of educational functions.

Although the lore surrounding curriculum guides usually suggests that they are not valued or used by teachers, their political significance makes them an important aspect of schooling. Through guides, schools communicate the intended curriculum. Perhaps it is because of the limitations noted here that teachers do not use them more frequently in their classroom planning. A fruitful place for your faculty to begin to grapple with what your curriculum ought to be could be an in-depth consideration of the relevant state and district curriculum guides. Their limitations ought to be overcome through modifications and adaptations for your school, based upon the input of all your faculty members. The modification of a curriculum guide to meet the expectations of your faculty could be a productive task in curriculum improvement. If it results in a clearer vision of what your faculty believes the intended curriculum ought to be, perhaps it will be used more often by your teachers as a guide for improving classroom practices.

SELECTION OF CONTENT AND LEARNING MATERIALS

Another way to study the intended curriculum is to analyze the learning materials teachers use and outlines of the content they select or develop for use in their classrooms. The materials selected or developed at your school, in fact, are probably a more precise indicator of what is expected — and likely — to be taught than are the preferred and perceived educational functions of your school or the statements of what ought to be taught contained in curriculum guides. Learning materials structure in very powerful ways the teacher/student interaction and usually determine the substance of what students learn.

All elementary teachers in the Study of Schooling sample were asked to submit examples of the materials they used in their classrooms. More specifically, they were asked to list the topics and skills they taught and the textbooks they used. They were requested to include the behavioral objectives that guided their practice, the tests they gave, the work sheets they used, and the homework they assigned. These materials were then analyzed for the six major subject areas in the elementary school curriculum: language arts and reading, mathematics, social studies, science, the arts, and physical education.

As was true of the curriculum guides, there was no way to determine whether the materials submitted were representative of the entire sample, but there was a large quantity of them. Although the quality and quantity of the materials sent by individual teachers varied, once again, the repetitiveness of many of the materials quickly became obvious as the analysis proceeded (Benham, 1978).

Language Arts and Reading

Language arts was the dominant curricular area for the classrooms in this sample of 13 elementary schools, as indicated by the quantity of materials the teachers submitted. Instruction in the language arts was either correlated with or integrated into the other subject areas. Topics most likely to be included were the basic language skills of reading, writing (composition and handwriting), speaking, and listening. Spelling, letter writing, use of the dictionary, and parts of speech were also frequently listed. Creative writing was listed occasionally. Skills taught tended to be the technical ones of correct language usage, rather than the development of higher intellectual abilities or skills of self-expression.

Teachers appeared to test students on low-level cognitive skills (e.g., identify the preposition, circle the verb, alphabetize words, correct the punctuation and capitalization, and match the phrase to its contraction). The weekly spelling test was still a part of how teachers evaluated student learning. Testing, however, did not appear to be as strongly emphasized in the elementary school as it was at the higher levels of schooling. Perhaps spending the entire school day together reduced the need for teachers to assess student learning formally through tests. It was interesting to note that, among the teachers who honored our request for samples of learning materials, only one included any behavioral objectives in them. Judging from this, students had little access to what specifically they were to learn, in advance of doing what was required in the materials. The textbook, however, was very strongly represented as a learning tool, with the products of the major publishing companies prominently featured. Only one teacher noted that no text in language arts was used. Supplementary materials included dictionaries, commercially prepared work sheets, newspapers, and, occasionally, educational television.

Most of the schools in our sample considered reading and language arts to be a single subject. However, reading materials were analyzed separately, since teachers themselves frequently treated reading as a separate subject from language arts. Reading was, of course, a fundamental part of the curriculum for every teacher. Reading instruction at the early elementary level differed from the upper grades. The early grades emphasized the basic skills in reading, while in the upper grades the focus shifted to remediation. In the materials the teachers submitted, the topics usually listed fell into categories of general skills, while specific skills listed at our request were simply more detailed descriptions of the general skills or topics. For example, phonics was listed as a topic, and word-attack skills were listed as specific skills. Tests included were usually those from commercial materials, although those teacher-made tests that were sent were similar to those in the language arts.

Mathematics

Materials submitted by teachers in mathematics were not significantly different in type from those in language arts and reading. Topics listed were broad ones such as numeration, addition, subtraction, multiplication, division, fractions, measurement, and geometry. Little distinction was made by teachers between topics and skills. The same topics and skills in math appeared for each grade level, with only a slight increase apparent in the level of difficulty. Basic texts were listed frequently, and the use of work sheets was universal. Tests given emphasized computation and word problems.

Social Studies

The pattern of the learning materials in the other subject areas differed somewhat from that in mathematics and language arts and reading. In the social studies, for example, there clearly was greater variety in the topics listed for the lower grades. Different cultures, basic needs of humans, natural resources, conservation, city problems, and careers illustrate this variety. By the time students reached the upper grades, however, the traditional subject areas in the social studies — history and geography — had become dominant. Teachers tended to list more complex skills in the social studies and few basic skills. Respect for cultural differences was a commonly listed skill, for example. Fewer tests were given in all grades in the social studies, with oral testing noted only in the earliest grades. Short essay tests began to appear at about the fifth-grade level.

Science

Since few teachers submitted materials in science, it appeared that science may not have been included as part of the curriculum by many teachers. Among the materials that were sent, no clear pattern of topics defined the curriculum for each grade level. A topic such as the solar system may have appeared at both the second- and fifth-grade levels. From the materials submitted, it was not clear that a topic that reappeared at the higher grade levels was likely to have been studied in more complex ways; that is, it might have been studied as mere repetition of earlier work. From the skills listed, however, science in the primary grades appeared to differ from that in the upper grades, when it was a part of the curriculum. Primary-level teachers seemed to emphasize the child in the world of science, that is, personal orientation in time and space and the natural order of living things. Upper-level teachers, on the other hand, showed a shift toward emphasizing the problem-solving method and a more objective view of science. Both groups seemed to be laying the groundwork in their science curricula for the development of higher intellectual skills.

Tests were not given frequently in science, but, when they were given, they were fairly traditional and tested recall of information. For teachers who taught science, textbooks were as common a curriculum tool as in the other curricular areas already discussed.

Arts

In the arts curriculum, there appeared to be considerably less use of commercially prepared materials, with texts in music being the exception. The arts seemed to be a part of the curriculum at all grade levels, but often in a very rudimentary form. Common topics listed were types of art expression, such as ballet, puppetry, crayon art, murals, and singing. Somewhat less common topics were seasonal experiences, the human body, insects, and home and family life. Elements of art and music such as color, design, harmony, melody, and rhythm were also listed. The skills listed emphasized techniques and self-expression skills. Tests were rarely mentioned. Evaluation was based on participation and sometimes on the analysis of the product or performance. Occasionally the arts were said to be integrated into or correlated with other subjects.

Physical Education

Materials and content submitted as representative of physical education were very limited, to the extent that it was not clear that some schools even had a physical education curriculum. As with arts instruction, there were far fewer commercially prepared materials. In those few packets submitted, organized sports were dominant, with health, safety, nutrition, drugs, and physical fitness also mentioned.

Conclusions

Even though many teachers in this sample of schools did not honor our request for their learning materials and content, the repetitiveness of what was submitted gave some clues about the answer to the question of what was to be taught. For example, in most subject areas, there appeared to be more similarity than variation in the topics and skills chosen at different schools. Although higher-order intellectual skills appeared in lists of concepts to be taught, the tests actually developed for the various subject areas evaluated the students on their recall of information much more than on their thinking abilities. The materials and content submitted — or not submitted, as in science, the arts, and physical education — raise the question of the extent to which these subject areas were, indeed, a part of the curriculum. (We will return to this question in chapter 3.) Although materials as such would not necessarily figure prominently in those subject areas, teachers still did not list the content or skills they were trying to teach in them. Language arts and reading clearly were the major thrusts in the curriculum of these elementary schools, as reflected in the quantity of materials sent to us.

The conclusions reached by this analysis of curriculum materials reinforced those reached as a result of the analysis of curriculum guides. The content to be taught was familiar and traditional. There was a clear, if not an exclusive, emphasis upon cognition; and students were tested on low-level cognitive skills, primarily recall of information. The strong role of reading and language arts and the lack of materials and content submitted in science, the arts, and physical education showed that the desire for a comprehensive curriculum, as reflected in teachers', students', and parents' stated preferences for a range of educational emphases, was not being met. Rather, the curriculum often seemed to be rather limited in scope and even ignored some areas that respondents had stated ought to be taught in these schools.

The role of learning materials in determining what students will learn is very powerful. An analysis of what they reflect could be a very productive way for your faculty to examine the intended curriculum of your school. The use of textbooks, work sheets, tests, handouts, homework, and even the occasional filmstrip and movie will structure how students and teachers interact and define what students have the opportunity to learn.

Some very specific questions you may want to raise with your faculty are

- Do the learning materials used by your faculty reflect what is generally considered to be important and what has been determined as desirable by your parents, administrators, teachers, and students? If not, how can you close the gap and thus improve the curriculum?
- Are the goals and specific objectives for each of the subject areas adequately represented in the kinds of materials your students use?

- Do the learning materials foster higher levels of thinking and problem solving or only emphasize the lower levels of recall and recognition?
- Is the affective development of students given attention, in addition to the cognitive development?
- Do the materials reflect an attempt to help students integrate the various subject areas whenever possible? For example, do the math materials support in appropriate ways the science content and skills being taught?
- Are additional materials needed for topics which you think it is important to study from an integrated, multidisciplinary approach — topics such as ecology or cultural studies?

By answering these types of questions, your faculty should become much clearer not only about how the content and materials used help define the intended curriculum, but what other types of materials need to be located or developed in order to support all areas of the intended curriculum.

SOURCES OF INFLUENCE OVER INSTRUCTIONAL CONTENT

The decisions teachers make about what they will teach are not arrived at in a vacuum devoid of influences. They plan in relation to legal requirements, pressure groups, their perceptions of students, their own knowledge and abilities, and expectations of significant groups concerned about schooling. They also bring their own interests and past experiences to bear in making decisions about what should be taught. Knowing how your teachers react to these various sources of influence is an important factor in establishing the intended curriculum.

Elementary teachers in the Study of Schooling sample were asked to rate 11 different sources of potentially considerable influence over the intended curriculum. For each major subject area they taught, the teachers were asked to indicate on a scale ranging from "a lot" to "none" how much influence each source had on what they taught. The 11 sources were as follows: district consultants; state- or district-recommended textbooks; state curriculum guides; district curriculum guides; commercially prepared materials; the teacher's own background, interests, and experiences; other teachers; students' interests and abilities; parent advisory councils; state equivalency exams; and teachers' unions. Although the number of teachers who responded to each of the six subject areas differed in each case the numbers were large (Klein, 1980b).

The two sources of greatest influence across all of the subject areas were the teacher's own background, interests, and experiences, and the students' interests and abilities. Two-thirds or more of the elementary teachers responded that these two sources of influence had "some" or "a lot" of influence over what they taught. By contrast, four of the sources were consistently rated as low in influence across all subject areas: district consultants, parent advisory councils, state equivalency exams, and teachers' unions.

The remaining five sources varied by subject area as to how much influence each had over what the teachers taught. State and district curriculum guides were rated as having moderate influence for most of the subject areas. The two exceptions to this were that both types of guides were perceived to have low influence in the arts, and state guides were reported to be of low influence in science.

State- or district-recommended textbooks varied considerably by subject area as to the amount of their reported influence. Not surprisingly, texts in reading/language arts and math were considered to be of high influence, while texts in science and social studies were of moderate influence and texts in the arts and physical education were of low influence. The latter two areas were hardly surprising, as comparatively few texts even exist in either of these subjects for the elementary school.

Other commercially prepared materials, however, seemed to be of somewhat greater influence. Again, in reading/language arts and math they were perceived to have high influence, as well as in science and social studies. For the arts and physical education, commercial materials other than texts were said to be of moderate influence.

A final source of influence, other teachers, also varied by subject area in the amount of perceived impact. Other teachers were reported to be of high influence for the arts and reading/language arts and of moderate influence over the other four subject areas.

It appears, then, that the number of sources of influence over what was taught was rather limited and constricted. The teachers themselves and their students consistently influenced what was taught to a large degree in each subject area. It could be expected, then, that the curriculum from classroom to classroom would vary to about the same degree as those two sources of influence varied. One would expect that there would be quite a lot of difference, yet the materials the teachers submitted contradicted that expectation. Something seemed to happen which mediated those influences and produced a much more conforming curriculum. (We will discuss further the need for greater variety in learning materials in the next chapter.) Perhaps rather than having their own personal background and experiences as the referents in responding to this item, teachers were using their professional background and experiences. This could help explain why the curriculum from school to school was so similar. Unfortunately, our data did not distinguish between these two possible interpretations. It seems plausible that teachers screened out their personal background and experiences and responded only to their professional preparation and background as sources of influence over what they taught. This would be an important distinction for you to make if you study this source of potential influence over the intended curriculum.

But what about student interests and abilities? If these were really sources of great influence, they, too, should have made the curriculum quite different from classroom to classroom. Since our evidence shows that, in fact, the intended curriculum and actual classroom practices were depressingly the same from school to school and classroom to classroom, we must ask the following questions:

- What caused such uniformity and stagnation in the curriculum?
- Was it the power of the traditional, commonly accepted curriculum?
- Could it have been that the pressure to have students achieve on standardized tests forced the conformity we saw?
- Were the texts used a factor in keeping the curriculum from school to school so similar?
- Was it the failure of curriculum guides to offer teachers help with individualization?
- What other factors might have kept teachers from using the diverse interests and abilities of students in modifying and adapting their curriculum?

These are the types of fundamental questions that need examining when your school investigates the potential sources of influence on the intended curriculum.

It is curious to note that two sources were reported to be of low influence which might legitimately have been expected to have significant influence: district consultants and parent advisory councils. It is reasonable to expect that district consultants would be used regularly by teachers to improve their curriculum and instruction. Consultants are expected to be very knowledgeable about the latest trends and techniques, as well as being experienced practitioners. Why, then, were they perceived to be of low influence in all subject areas by our sample of elementary teachers? Perhaps their job descriptions, their preparation for the job, or the way they spend their time should be revised so as to be of greater service to teachers. An important question for you to explore is how helpful consultants are to your teachers and what might be impeding their greater potential usefulness.

In recent years there has been considerable discussion about involving parents more in their children's education. It appears, however, that if parent involvement occurred in this sample of schools, it was not influential on what teachers sought to teach. And yet, where could parents be better involved than in a broad definition of the intended curriculum? Deciding at a broad level what functions your school should serve and what should be taught are ways in which an advisory council might make a significant contribution to the school. Although we talk a lot about it and few debate that it *should* happen, we still know very little about *how* to involve a parent advisory council meaningfully in life at school. Hence, our efforts have been ineffective.

The remaining sources of at least moderate influence would seem to be yet another factor in reinforcing a very traditional interpretation of what should be taught: textbooks, other commercial materials, state and district guides, and, for most subject areas, other teachers. Perhaps these sources of influence acted in combination to overrule influences for diversity, thus producing the overwhelming similarities in the curriculum.

The following are some questions that could be raised with your faculty, in addressing these complex interactions.

- What potential influences on the intended curriculum do your teachers respond to and/or ignore?
- What are the implications of each of these sources of influence?
- How do they impact the curriculum? Do they make it more uniform or more unique from classroom to classroom?
- Do your teachers feel under any undue pressure to respond to a particular influence? Are there any that are too powerful in their influence on the curriculum such as teachers' unions or parents who may attempt to censor the curriculum?
- Are your teachers aware of sources of influence that can provide ideas and support for their curriculum, such as district guides and consultants?

Perhaps a deliberate effort needs to be made to decrease the impact of some influences while increasing others.

Your school faculty may well respond quite differently from our sample of schools. The issue, however, is of basic importance to the school curriculum. Each source has the potential of influencing the intended curriculum in important ways. When you have identified which influences your faculty is most responsive to, why, and to what end, you will want to ask whether their pattern of responses reflects how you would like the influences to be. If not, how do they need to change?

ISSUES TO BE CONSIDERED IN THE INTENDED CURRICULUM

The preceding discussion of our data raises fundamental questions for your faculty to discuss in their determination of what the intended curriculum will be. Each category of data reported and discussed is an important component, and any one could be a starting point for you in developing a framework for curriculum improvement.

Without a unified framework and vision for what the curriculum ought to be for your school, one that is coherent within and across grade levels, teachers do their planning in isolation and in uninformed ways. The results may or may not contribute to the broad functions and goals your school may have. With such a framework and vision, however, each teacher can find unique and personalized ways for his or her classroom curriculum to support overall goals.

There are some issues and topics that are imbedded within the data previously reported, which ought to be discussed by your faculty before making firm decisions about what the intended curriculum of your school will be. Four have already been mentioned but will be highlighted here as possible topics for your faculty to discuss: (1) the match between the sources of influence on the intended curriculum and the vision for your school, (2) what is to be taught, (3) individualization and personalization of the curriculum, and (4) the role of the teacher.

The Match Between Sources of Influence and Your Vision

The data reported for the Study of Schooling sample strongly suggest that what was being taught was the traditional content of the subject areas. The concepts, skills, and topics included in the curriculum guides and the materials and content the teachers submitted to us contained little that was new. Throughout the grades, they were reflective of the disciplines and contained content that has been a part of the curriculum for years. Teachers continued to teach word-attack skills, computational skills, the solar system, the family, sports, and "crayon art." The longevity of this type of curricular content undoubtedly says something about the importance attributed to it. Apparently there are many who would not want students to leave elementary school without those abilities and some knowledge of those topics. But it also may say much more about the power of tradition and convenience in the curriculum. These topics and activities are entrenched in the curriculum because few have been able to imagine them being replaced or at least augmented by other important learning.

If these topics also represent the curriculum at your school, some fundamental questions must be raised about your intended curriculum: When will your students learn about themselves; about how to get along with others and resolve conflict? When will they develop learning skills? When will they learn about the importance of protecting the environment; about the interdependence of people and all forms of life? When will they learn to address pressing societal problems, such as prejudice, inequality, and pollution? These are content areas that appeared infrequently, if at all, in the intended curriculum of our sample. Moreover, they are not likely to be addressed well by the traditional organization of content found in our sample of schools. Yet, if you really want a balanced curriculum, these topics are as essential as those traditionally found in the curriculum.

The vision that our sample of parents, teachers, and students had, as defined at least in part by the educational functions they wanted their schools to meet, went beyond the traditional view of the curriculum as reflected in the guides, work sheets, tests, and texts of the schools. The social, personal, and vocational goals they wanted will not be met successfully through the type of intended curriculum defined by the curriculum guides, the traditional content, the learning materials used, and the acknowledged influences upon the teachers. A more balanced curriculum will require other curriculum designs than just the traditional subject-matter one (Klein, 1986). It will be necessary to introduce topics that cut across subject areas and processes that are fundamental to critical thinking and problem solving in many situations. Their view will require improved curriculum guides, bold curriculum planning, additional materials to be used in their schools, and better understanding about the potential impact of conservative sources of influence over the curriculum. These additions and modifications would do much to help the intended curriculum of this group of schools more closely match the vision of what was wanted.

This suggests an important area of discussion for your faculty. Do the components of the intended curriculum for your school match the vision you hold for your school? Is there a close congruence between what is desired and what is actually guiding the intended curriculum? In order for your curriculum to have the kind of impact you want upon the students, you must have a good match in these areas and between them and actual practices in your school and classrooms. Research suggests that this match is not as close as would be desirable (Goodlad et al., 1974).

Careful deliberation about the match among the components of your intended curriculum is essential to curriculum improvement. These decisions must not be left up to tradition or be imposed upon you by external sources. They must be made *by* your faculty and *for* your school. How well all of these aspects fit with one another is an important barometer of the health of your institution and the degree of satisfaction that your constituents feel for your school.

What Should Be Taught

Clearly, any elementary school curriculum must undergo close scrunity as our society changes. To perpetuate the status quo in curriculum is not adequate for the changing times. Traditional answers to what should be taught must no longer be accepted as "givens." They must be augmented by other functions and goals of the curriculum which are also viewed as important to our world today. New criteria must be developed, in order to keep the curriculum current and relevant. The curriculum must contain new goals and focus on how to learn, how to use technology for human benefit, how to solve problems, where to locate resources, how to relate to people and the environment, and how to help students understand themselves better, in addition to the perennial basics. These are goals that represent skills that students must have if they are to function adequately in today's society. To include these additional goals will require different ways of conceptualizing and organizing the curriculum (Klein, 1986). New expectations must be created about how the curriculum can help students learn and develop essential traits for living in a complex, rapidly changing society.

The answer you provide to the question of what should be taught is as fundamental to curriculum improvement as food is to life. The functions, goals, objectives, materials, content, and forms of evaluation you decide upon must help equip your students to cope successfully with our world in the 21st century. What is to be taught in the intended curriculum must be carefully defined, and then practices must be monitored by all to assure that what is to be taught is what your students really need and what they are actually getting in their elementary school experiences. Those determinations are at the heart of your curriculum improvement plan.

Individualization and Personalization of the Curriculum

The standardization and lack of individualization in many curricula are issues that your faculty should also address and resolve through careful deliberation, since these, too, have great significance for your students and our society. What was taught in this sample of schools was a common curriculum with surprisingly little variation from classroom to classroom or school to school. Where variation was found, the differences were more superficial than fundamental.

Is there such fundamental content for the elementary school that all students should be expected to learn it? For most of us, the answer is yes. There are basic skills, processes, and attitudes that are essential if a student is to continue learning and to function effectively in a multicultural, democratic, technological society. These include learning to read, write, and compute; to think critically; to weigh evidence; to make skillful and thoughtful observations and take informed actions about one's physical and social environment; to appreciate the cultural diversity of our society; to learn how to learn; and to accept the interdependence of human beings on this planet. The elementary school experience must contribute to learning in these areas, much more than the intended curriculum of this sample of schools did.

Even those aspects of the elementary school curriculum that must be taught to all students, however, can be taught in much more individualized ways than they were in our sample. There are alternatives to the typical pattern of direct instruction to the total class (Goodlad, 1984). Even though the same content must be learned, your students now have options as to when and how they learn it. Computer-assisted instruction is a reality for many classrooms and students. It can be independent of total-group instruction and used as an important alternative way for students to learn what they must. Similarly, alternative activities and teaching strategies can be used to meet more effectively the varying learning styles and needs of your students. Learning resources must be selected on the basis of how well they help your students learn what they need to in a variety of ways. This kind of curriculum planning can help to individualize the curriculum and more adequately meet the needs of all your students.

There can also be considerable diversity in the topics and concepts used in learning the basic skills, processes, and attitudes. In learning how to learn, for example, does it matter greatly whether your students learn about astronomy, geology, sociology, or biology? Many concepts and procedures within these fields are important to learn about, but every student cannot — and should not — be expected to learn them all. Subject-area choices could be made by students if the curricular emphasis remained on the development of basic skills in learning how to learn rather than knowledge of particular content. The specific content could be adapted to student interests, which increases the chances of students' needs being met, provides a higher degree of motivation for learning, and assures curiosity for continued learning.

To personalize the curriculum means to provide opportunities for students to choose what is of interest to them, in addition to learning what they must. This means enabling students to select at some time in their classrooms what they want to learn, whether anyone else is interested in the topic or not. The standardized curriculum for all students is an important component of the intended curriculum, but it must not be all that students have the opportunity to learn while they are in school. The personalization of the curriculum recognizes that our knowledge is now so extensive that there must be opportunities for students to choose what they are interested in and want to pursue. Learning resources must also be provided in the classroom for students to have this opportunity. Thus, both personalization and individualization of the curriculum are important attributes of a balanced curriculum.

If your curriculum is to have more diversity — more individualization and personalization — materials must be selected or developed to help in these efforts, and teachers must be encouraged to reorganize their classrooms as needed to encourage students to learn about different topics and concepts. It may be desirable, for example, for you to have fewer textbooks in science and social studies and many more inexpensive supplementary paperback booklets and magazines on a variety of reading levels. Within this format, the topics your students select could range from dinosaurs to the solar system, from rocks to space travel, from problems of growing up to problems of the aged, and from traditional lifestyles to new social mores. Computer software could also be selected to help meet the requirements of your personalized and individualized curriculum. These resources would provide students with greater opportunities for pursuing their own interests. This will mean more student movement and noisier classrooms. Teachers will need to have the skills to interact with large groups, small groups, and individuals; to be able to select a variety of effective materials; to have the ability to coordinate the learning of all the students within various groups; and to be continuously aware of student interests and needs. To engage in these tasks will require new skills on the part of your teachers and new expectations of classroom practices on the part of the administrators at your school.

New Roles for Teachers

The curriculum we found in our sample of schools reflected the basic assumption that teachers should function as conveyors of information and students will learn what is presented in much the same way as sponges soak up water. Yet the broad vision our constituent groups had for the type of curriculum they wanted suggested other roles for teachers. In a balanced curriculum teachers must be skilled as role models in social interaction, as listeners and resources for students having problems, as coordinators of resources for students investigating real problems in their communities, and as friends who care about individual students. To what extent are your teachers prepared to take on expanded roles, if they are required in the curriculum your constituents desire? Are they attached to their roles as simply conveyors of information, or are they willing to take on new roles that are yet ill defined and perhaps even threatening? Your teachers must be prepared through staff development programs to perform complex and varied roles, if a balanced, relevant curriculum is to be implemented.

Further, it must be asked whether the role of conveyor of information is even an acceptable or desirable one for your teachers, given the fact that our society finds itself in an information revolution. It is very possible that the computer will perform this role better than the human teacher in the future, making available to students a very broad array of content whenever they need it. This will free up teachers to perform more intellectually complex and less mechanical roles than those associated with conveyors of facts and details. The information society into which we are moving is forcing us to create new and more vital roles for teachers, as computers become more common in and important to the education of our students.

How your faculty responds to this mandate will be an important determinant of your intended curriculum. Teachers must be expected by administrators and assisted through staff development efforts to become curriculum developers, not mere users of textbooks. With these new skills, the curriculum of the classroom will become more responsive to the interests of students and teachers and more conducive to helping students acquire the broad array of knowledge, skills, and attitudes the elementary school ought to focus upon as "basic" education.

Perhaps the most fundamental issue regarding the role of teachers is how to support their work as curriculum decision makers, not just as curriculum users. Teachers' creativity has great potential for improving the curriculum in dramatic ways. Teachers must learn about and become skillful in relating what they do in their classrooms to the development of all the human traits, knowledge, attitudes, and skills they hope for in the schooling process. Your teachers must, in essence, become skilled curriculum decision makers at the classroom level.

Help in doing this must come from a variety of sources, and costs must be acknowledged and the necessary resources must be allocated. Skills must continue to be developed through staff development activities; through meetings among your teachers at optimal times; through hiring consultants to meet with your faculty to examine critically what they are doing in relation to what they want to do; through the necessary financial resources being provided; through the cooperation, support, and involvement of your administration and lay groups; and through time provided for the ongoing critical analysis of their classroom work by the teachers themselves. The assistance given them must be on a continuous basis so that your teachers will learn to provide diverse classroom activities in order to achieve a variety of outcomes.

Although the teachers in this sample perceived themselves as active curriculum developers to some degree, they seemed to have few resources and limited skills for this important role. Even curriculum guides written to help them cast them as curriculum users more than curriculum developers. This distinction is an important one. The roles are different; the skills needed are different. If your teachers are to function as true professionals, they must have the necessary skills to plan, implement, and evaluate curriculum, to be full participants in the curriculum development cycle.

Teachers are, indeed, primary participants in curriculum development, whether they have the needed skills and resources or not. To become the professional educators they are expected to be, your teachers must have the abilities needed to engage in curriculum development as skilled and continuous participants. Not to assure that your teachers are curriculum developers — that is, to restrict their role to mere users of curriculum — is to limit the promises of and hopes for what your students will gain from their schooling. To assist your teachers in becoming skilled and primary participants in curriculum development efforts is to help assure that your students will receive maximum assistance from your school in their growth and development as well-rounded human beings.

This important new role for teachers is a theme to which we will return in later chapters. With a new focus on the role of the teacher as a skilled curriculum decision maker in district staff development programs and the work of the local school faculty, the curriculum will likely become much more comprehensive and thus meet the additional needed and desired goals that appear to be receiving such scant attention in today's curriculum. Schooling, at the same time, will become more relevant to the lives of students outside of school and more interesting for the time they are in school. Finally, the impact of schooling would be longer lasting, focusing on aspects of development that are important throughout the lifespan.

CHAPTER 3

Classroom Practices

The preceding chapter focused on the intended curriculum, which consists of your expectations for what will be taught and your efforts at planning your curriculum, prior to engagement in the classroom. Do not overlook the political importance of the intended curriculum, although you may wonder about its practical importance as you expend efforts and resources to develop it. The intended curriculum is a public, political statement of your vision and intentions and as such is a basic definition of your curriculum. It becomes very powerful when you use it in making decisions about classroom practices. Resources are purchased, teachers are selected, schools and teachers are evaluated, space is allocated, and much committee work is done, all on the basis of the intended curriculum.

It is reasonable to expect that your carefully developed intended curriculum will guide your teachers in making their classroom decisions, for otherwise the expenditure of time, effort, and resources upon it would not be justified. Thus it has practical as well as political importance. As has been noted already, however, there is general acknowledgment that the intended curriculum is not always reflected in classroom practices. Indeed, there is an impressive body of research that indicates that the gap is significant (e.g., Goodlad, 1984; Goodlad et al., 1974). It complicates the assessment and improvement of classroom practice, especially when it becomes clear that the reasons for the discrepancy are sometimes good and sometimes bad.

Some of the factors that intervene to cause the adaptation and sometimes outright rejection of the intended curriculum as a guide to classroom practices include the complexity of guiding learning for numerous and diverse students; competing demands for classroom time; the teacher's own abilities, interests, and values; the teacher's perceptions of student abilities, interests, and needs; resources immediately available; and priorities established by the school. There is a host of other such variables.

The elementary school classroom is an incredibly complex educational setting. The ongoing work of the classroom demands frequent decision making on many levels. The kinds of decisions that relate to curriculum include, for example, which subjects to teach at what times during the day, how long the lesson will last, which students get grouped together for a lesson, the minute-to-minute monitoring of how well students are learning, how many days a week science or art will be taught (if at all), what type of activity will be offered to students, how the immediate activity must be modified to keep students learning, and which materials will be used. An understanding of the contribution that such decisions make to the atmosphere of a classroom and their power to determine what students will actually learn is fundamental to curriculum improvement; in fact, curriculum reform will not work without it. You must not minimize the need to attend to classroom practices, in spite of the difficulties involved.

This chapter discusses the research data related to selected classroom practices that are representative of basic curricular concerns. Our discussion here is based upon data collected from the individual classrooms of our sample of schools. We will focus on the following four aspects of how time is spent: allocation of time to various subjects; teacher time spent on preparation for the different subject areas; time students were expected to spend on homework; and class time spent on instruction, behavior control, and routines. We will also examine six specific instructional practices and take a look at the teacher's use of learning principles; the types of classroom activities provided; and the appropriateness of learning materials and content. In the final section we will highlight some of the major issues in classroom practice. This chapter will help you to understand more fully the relationships between classroom practices and the intended curriculum. The data will become even more meaningful after you have collected data from your own classrooms and compared it with our data. Then you will be ready to examine your data for their potential implications for curriculum improvement at your school.

HOW TIME WAS SPENT

One of the issues discussed in chapter 2 was that of the comprehensive or balanced curriculum, that is, the scope or breadth of the curriculum in terms of the functions and goals of the school. You were encouraged to decide whether your intended curriculum will have a narrowly defined scope in terms of a few academic subjects, highly selected functions and goals, and limited topics or processes; or whether it will be broad in nature and encompass many subjects, a variety of functions and goals, and diverse topics and processes. From the evidence presented in the last chapter, it became apparent that the intended curriculum in our sample of elementary schools was quite restricted. But the evidence was based largely on broad curricular planning, not the daily practices of the classrooms. What can be learned about the curriculum from the specifics of classroom practice? One very basic concern and a very popular way of judging the quality of curriculum and instruction is the use of time. How time is allocated and spent in the classroom is a major factor in determining the curriculum and has great impact upon what students will learn. A variety of data were collected about this curriculum element from the Study of Schooling sample.

Classroom Time Allocated to Subject Areas

Teachers were asked to estimate the approximate percentage of classroom time that was spent on instruction, by subject area, per week. Across all 13 elementary schools in our sample, reading/language arts clearly dominated the curriculum (see Table 3.1). On the average, instruction in this subject area accounted for over $1^{1}/_{2}$ hours of the school day. This finding supports a similar one based on the curriculum materials analysis discussed in the preceding chapter: Reading/language arts was the major curriculum thrust for these elementary schools. As might be expected, math was allocated the next highest percentage of time, enough to amount to slightly under 1 hour per day. The remaining subject areas were estimated by the teachers to be well under 1 hour of instruction per day. The arts were given third highest estimated time, followed by social studies, science, and physical education.

Table 3.1 Analysis of Classroom Time Spent on Instruction, by Subject Area, per Week

	Teachers' Estimates		Observers' Data
	% Weekly	Hours/Week	% Weekly[b]
Reading/Language Arts	34	7.54	51
Math	19	4.5	14
Arts[a]	15	3.33	5
Social Studies	12	2.77	8
Science	10	2.28	5
Physical Education	8	1.89	n.a.[c]

Source: J. Wright, 1980b

[a]Figures given here combine the teachers' separate estimates for art, music, dance, and drama.
[b]Observers' percentages do not add up to 100% because other activities were also being monitored.
[c]Observers' data for physical education were not included in the research report.

Totaling the teachers' estimates yields an average of 4¹/₂ hours per day spent on instruction in the various subjects. (The adequacy of this will be discussed later.) The question must be raised, of course, about how accurate these estimates are in relation to the perceptions of others. As Table 3.1 shows, our data suggest that the teachers' estimates were compatible with those of others.

Observers spent 3 full days in selected classrooms, studying time allocations from their perspective and in more detail than was possible via the questionnaires given to students and teachers. Because of the cost of having a trained observer spend considerable time in a single classroom, not all classrooms in the 13-school sample could be studied in this way. Two classrooms at each grade level (1 through 6) were observed in every elementary school.

For each selected classroom, the observers were asked to note every 5 minutes the subject area of instruction (physical education was not included in this summary). Based upon this observation data, the emphasis was strongly upon reading/language arts for grades 1 through 6 — about half of all the lessons observed were in that area (see Table 3.1). Math was again the second most often observed subject area, though it accounted for less than 1 lesson out of every 5; social studies, less than 1 lesson out of every 10; and the arts and science, about 1 lesson in every 20, each. It is clear that the opportunity for students to be engaged in a lesson in any subject area other than reading/language arts and math decreased rather dramatically. It should also be noted that observers' estimates for percentage of time allocated to the arts, social studies, and science vary significantly from the teachers'. For example, teachers estimated 15% of classroom time was devoted to the arts, while observers' estimates averaged only 5%. The reason for this discrepancy in estimates is not clear. It is possible that observers did not appear in the classrooms on the days art was scheduled and that to the teachers, art was a more important subject area in terms of time allocated than our observers saw.

These estimates of how time was spent on the different subject areas indicated a strong, and in my judgment excessive, emphasis on reading/language arts. This undoubtedly has come about because of the belief that reading is such a basic tool to all other learning that its development is a particularly essential mission of the elementary school. Moreover, standardized test scores emphasize these skills, and schools and teachers are held accountable for student achievement on these tests. No one can argue with these reasons. What must be assessed, however, is what your students will not have the opportunity to learn in other subject areas if such limited time is spent on them. Such use of time creates an imbalanced curriculum. Other important goals of your intended curriculum may well be slighted or ignored with this kind of skewed emphasis upon reading/language arts. This issue will be explored further at the conclusion of this chapter.

Time Teachers Spent on Subject-Area Preparation

Another important aspect of the use of time in relation to the curriculum was the time teachers spent in preparing for each subject area. Teachers were asked to estimate this in terms of hours per week. Not surprisingly, the rank ordering of subject areas is similar to the other two estimates of time just discussed. On average, teachers spent $2^1/_2$ hours per week on planning instruction in reading/language arts; approximately 2 hours for math; $1^1/_2$ hours each for social studies, science, and the arts; and about 1 hour for physical education (Tye, 1979f).

The previously established relative importance of the different subject areas is thus reinforced by varying the amounts of time spent on planning and preparing for instruction in each. Preparation for reading/language arts received almost twice as much time as preparation in any other subject area except math. Preparation for reading/language arts and math combined took up $4^1/_2$ hours, almost half the total of 10 hours teachers spent on preparation for all subjects. Again, this distribution of planning time does not reflect the balanced curriculum that was desired by most of these same teachers, their students, and the students' parents, as reported in the preceding chapter. It is clear that some important goals of the curriculum will not be well served by this skewed use of time in preparing for lessons.

Time Students Were Expected to Spend on Homework

We examined a different aspect of time for learning by asking the teachers to estimate how much time they expected students to spend each day on homework for all the subjects combined. Homework is usually perceived as a time for practicing or extending what has been taught in the classroom and as such is considered an important part of time spent in learning, even though it is done beyond the classroom setting.

The elementary teachers reported they expected students to do homework for slightly less than half an hour per night (Tye, 1979e). Further information about the quality of these assignments would help put this estimate of time into perspective, but our study did not include such questions. This would be an important area for your faculty to explore, however. You might ask if the homework assigned by your teachers consists of "drill-and-grill" exercises. That is the approach we might assume, based upon the analysis of the type of class assignments as discussed in the preceding chapter. Other possibilities include creative writing, critiqueing TV specials, organizing reports, and interviewing community leaders. These are very different types of homework activities, and they might significantly extend the work of the classroom.

In any form, homework assignments should extend the work of the classroom in meaningful ways and be relevant to curriculum goals. Given the current push for more homework in order to upgrade the quality of the schools, the 30-minute expectation would seem to be reasonable to some and perhaps minimal to others. This kind of judgment can be made on a more informed basis if you know what type of homework your students are asked to do. More drill is not necessarily better; it should be assigned only to students who could benefit from it, and never to all students just to keep them busy. Some types of homework, such as those mentioned above, however, can be profitable to all students.

Time Teachers Spent on Instruction, Behavior, and Routines

Another important aspect of how time is spent in classrooms is the actual time allocated to instruction itself, across the subject areas. Just how much time does the teacher actually spend productively on instruction, compared to the amount of time spent handling routines, establishing control over the students, and discussing topics irrelevant to the lesson? Observers in A Study of Schooling estimated how time was spent within an instructional unit by recording every 5 minutes whether the teacher was (1) engaged in instruction; (2) engaged in classroom routines such as passing out supplies, taking attendance, or allowing students to sharpen pencils or get their books out; or (3) engaged in controlling the behavior of students. It should be emphasized that these estimates of time were based upon what the teacher was doing and were not measures of engaged time on the part of students, an area that has been defined and measured by other research studies (e.g., Denham & Lieberman, 1980).

As shown in Table 3.2, observers noted that elementary teachers devoted nearly three-quarters of their time to instruction and about one-fifth to attending to routines; the remaining time was mostly spent controlling the behavior of students in the classroom. This suggests that, contrary to the views of many critics of schools in general, the teachers

Table 3.2 Percentages of Classroom Time Spent in Three Areas

| | % of Classroom Time[a] | | |
Rater	Instruction	Routines	Behavior Control
Observers			
Early Elementary	73	19	6
Upper Elementary	73	21	4
Teachers	70	15	13

Source: J. Wright, 1980a

[a]Percentages do not add up to 100% across all three categories because raters perceived some small amounts of time spent on activity that did not fall into any of the three categories.

in this sample were devoting by far the major portion of their time to instruction. These proportions varied only slightly from the early to the upper elementary grades.

As another measure of this use of time, teachers themselves were asked to estimate the amount of daily class time they thought they spent on the same three categories: instruction, daily routines, and controlling students' behavior. This was a much grosser estimate of how time was spent in classrooms than what the observers recorded, but, overall, elementary teachers' estimates were remarkably close to the observers' findings (see Table 3.2). Teachers saw themselves spending by far the greatest percentage of time on instruction, with much less time spent on the other two categories. Both were also in general agreement on the amount of time spent on attending to routines. Interestingly, teachers estimated that more time was spent on getting students to behave than observers recorded in this category. There are several possible explanations for this discrepancy. First, there is a tendency for students to behave well when visitors are in the room, no matter how much the teacher tries to portray a "typical" time for the observers. Second, getting elementary school students to behave requires a considerable amount of time in the beginning and less time as the students become more mature and socialized into the ways of schooling; teachers would be more aware of this task over time and would therefore have higher estimates when compared with what observers saw in limited visitations. Still, teachers did not seem to "waste" significant amounts of time, if socialization is seen as an important aspect of schooling.

Students, too, were asked to estimate how they spent their time in classrooms. Early elementary students were asked simply to select whichever one of the three categories took the most time in their class: learning, passing out materials and taking attendance, or getting students to behave. Although less than half of the early elementary students thought they spent the most time on learning, it was still the category selected by the largest percentage of students (see Table 3.3).

Table 3.3 Percentages of Students Selecting Activity as
Most Time Consuming

	Most Time Consuming (%)[a]		
Rater	Instruction	Routines	Behavior Control
Early Elementary Students[a]	45	18	37
Upper Elementary Students[a]	53	14	32

Source: J. Wright, 1980a
[a]Student estimates were based on responses to the question, "Which takes the most time?"

Over a third of them thought the most time was spent on getting students to behave. It could be expected that more time might be spent in the early grades than in the upper grades on helping students conform to the demands of schooling and living as a group. However, as can be seen from the table, this was not the students' perception. Perhaps a more valid explanation of the rather large number of students giving top billing to this use of classroom time relates to the vividness of this category to the students. A powerful adult telling students when they are out of line or generally not doing what is expected of them may be threatening enough to make a stronger impression upon many young children than instruction. It is also likely that socialization into classroom life is difficult for a few students in every classroom. Helping these students adjust to the expected behaviors might have required considerable time and effort by the teacher. These students may need sustained attention in the elementary school since their problems may extend over several years. These encounters would undoubtedly be very vivid to all students and thus may account for the rather large number of students who thought the most time was spent on getting students to behave.

Finally, nearly a fifth of the early elementary students saw routines such as passing out materials and taking attendance as occupying the most class time. One wonders why any student would have this perception, since most teachers would try to keep such time to a minimum.

Upper elementary students were asked to estimate not only which of the three categories took the most time, but which took the next most, and which took the least. They were asked, in other words, to rank-order the three categories. Table 3.3 shows the percentages of students who ranked each category as the most time consuming. Learning was again perceived as taking up the most time, by slightly over half of the students, but nearly a third of the students thought most class time was spent on controlling behavior. Thus the difference between older and younger students on this dimension was surprisingly small; apparently, even in the upper grades many students continued to see behavioral control as a predominant use of classroom time.

The percentage of students selecting routines as the category taking up the most time also did not change much from the early to the upper grades. What specific factors in classroom living they were thinking of when they responded to these categories is not known, of course, but most educators would have hoped that the percentages of students who perceived the most time spent on either behavior or routines would have been lowered as the students progressed in school and that more students would have perceived learning as the major use of time in the classroom.

Although the ways in which the three different groups of participants in the study estimated the use of time in the classroom varied, there was consistency at least in the fact that the category of instruction and learning was perceived by students, teachers, and observers to account for more time than any other. This is a very important positive characteristic of these schools. By contrast, the adults, both observers and teachers, estimated that much less time was spent on getting students to behave than did the students themselves. A good percentage of students said this took up the most time, while teachers and observers estimated small percentages of time for controlling behavior. The basis of comparison is not exactly the same, but there is an interesting discrepancy here.

Should you discover a similar discrepancy, interviews with some of your students would be important in helping you to understand further the perceptions of students about the use of time in the classroom. The interviews could help you explore such questions as

- Is the time the teacher spends on student behavior really more vivid to elementary students?
- Does getting boisterous students to behave result in a change of activity in the classroom that grabs the interest of all students?
- Is learning how to behave in a group-oriented, public setting such an important task for elementary students that it might be considered by them to be a function of school, just as much as instruction in subject areas?

For some reason, getting students to behave was seen by them as consuming considerable classroom time in our sample. If it does in your school, too, it should be of interest for you to find out why.

The category of routines bears some similarity across the three groups, although, as noted earlier, the basis for comparison is not the same for adults and students. A teacher's estimation that 15% of classroom time is spent on routines is not the same as a student being among the 18% who see it as the single most time-consuming activity in the

classroom. A possible interpretation of the *trend* toward similar perceptions is that perhaps attending to routines is less personalized and less
vivid than when teachers work with students to get them to behave.

The way in which time is spent in classrooms is a very significant
factor, one that you need to examine closely as you work to improve your
curriculum. Your students spend a limited amount of time in school and
your teachers are expected — and want — to make good use of it. How
they spend the available time sets clear boundaries for how much and
what your students can learn. So far, however, the various estimates of
perceived use of time we have discussed have not addressed three related
issues regarding instructional time: what types of instructional practices
are used, what learning principles are utilized, and what kinds of classroom activities are engaged in during instruction. These should be of
primary importance to you as you investigate how time is spent in your
classrooms, and they are the topics to be discussed in the next sections of
this chapter.

INSTRUCTIONAL PRACTICES USED IN THE CLASSROOM

Data were collected by our observers on what types of instructional
practices were being used in the selected sample of elementary classrooms. Because the data for various aspects of A Study of Schooling
were not always collected in exactly the same way, there is more detail
reported here than in other sections. Observers recorded which of several teaching techniques were used during instruction and reported on
them in two different ways. First, every 5 minutes they noted any of six
types of techniques the teacher had used throughout that observation
period (hereafter called the FMI, for the five-minute-interval record).
From the FMIs, an estimate was made of the percentage of total instructional time for each of the techniques by averaging their use across
about 12 hours of observation per classroom (Sirotnik, 1981).

Second, every 15 minutes observers indicated the major technique
or activity that had been used predominantly during that period of
time. The results were called "classroom snapshot data." The overlap
and consistency between these two types of observation data establish
with a good degree of confidence the overall conclusions of the observations.

The six major types of teaching techniques recorded were:

1. Lecture, demonstrate, and explain
2. Observe and monitor

3. Question
4. Respond to students (acknowledge, reject, praise, give corrective feedback, and reprimand)
5. Discuss
6. Attend to routines

All are crucial behaviors on the part of a teacher. It is through their use that learning is guided and directed and, to a large degree, both the quality and quantity of instructional time in the classroom are determined. The estimated frequency of each of the different techniques is discussed below.

Lecturing, Demonstrating, and Explaining

A major teaching technique that every teacher uses is comprised of lecturing, demonstrating a skill or concept to students, and explaining some phenomenon to students. This was, in fact, the most commonly observed teaching technique throughout the elementary grades. The snapshot data reveal that teachers devote nearly a quarter of classroom instructional time to lecturing, demonstrating, or explaining to the students (see Table 3.4). This estimate was corroborated by the FMI data, which averaged 20.7% across all elementary grades.

Observing and Monitoring

Another important technique that teachers must use for productive learning is to observe and monitor student learning. As students explore and practice what they are learning on their own or in groups, the teacher must be sure that they are on target and engaging in the task correctly. From the FMI data, the estimate across all the elementary grades for this technique was 9.1% of the total instructional time. The snapshot data, however, indicated higher percentages of time spent on this technique, and showed a difference between the earlier grades and the upper grades that was larger than it was for lecturing (see Table 3.4). By inference, then, students were likely to be actively engaged in practicing what they were learning for this amount of time at a minimum, although they were likely to be engaged in such practice during the use of other instructional techniques, too.

Questioning

A third way in which teachers engage and direct student learning is by questioning them about what they are learning. Observers were

Table 3.4 Percentage of Teachers' Classroom Time Spent in Six Teaching Activities, Recorded by Observers

Teaching Activity	% of Classroom Time	
	Early Elementary	Upper Elementary
Lecturing, demonstrating, explaining	23.3[a]	24.7[a]
Observing and monitoring	14.9[a]	18.1[a]
Questioning	15.0	11.8
Directed	14.5	11.2
Open-ended	0.5	0.6
Responding to Students	13.7	12.2
To student-initiated questions	2.2	3.4
Refusing to respond	0.1	0.1
Neutral response	3.1	2.4
Praising	1.9	1.0
Reprimanding	0.4	0.4
Correcting	4.8	3.8
Correcting with guidance	1.4	1.2
Discussing	5.3	7.7
Attending to Routines	19.0	20.7
Preparation for learning (teacher)	9.6[a]	10.5[a]
Preparing, changing, cleaning up	11.9[a]	10.5[a]

Source: J. Wright, 1980a
[a]Snapshot data; all other figures are FMI data.

asked to record in the FMI data when two different types of questions were asked: direct questions that required a correct and focused response, and open-ended questions that allowed a less structured, more reflective response from students. The data reveal that teachers spent 11% to 15% of the instructional time asking students to respond to questions that called for a clear and focused response (see Table 3.4). By contrast, teachers spent less than 1% of the total instructional time asking students to respond to less structured and more reflective questions about what they were learning.

Responding to Students

Teachers must also respond to students during the course of instruction, in order to clarify any points of confusion for students, to reinforce what is being learned correctly, and to redirect what is being learned erroneously. This was the fourth category of instructional practices our observers recorded. Examples of this type of teacher behavior that observers looked for in the FMI were acknowledging, rejecting, praising, providing corrective feedback, or reprimanding a student. The teachers used a variety of different behaviors within this general technique for about 13% of the total instructional time (see Table 3.4).

Sometimes, however, students specifically asked for help from teachers on their own initiative, as instruction progressed. Observers recorded the student-initiated requests for help whenever they occurred during an FMI. Overall, teachers in the early grades gave only a very small percentage of time to responding directly and deliberately to student-initiated requests or questions during instruction; however, this was due to the infrequency of such requests, since, when made, they were very rarely denied or ignored.

The ways in which the teacher responds to students can have much influence over the quality of classroom instruction. Whether a student is praised or given some other type of positive response; simply acknowledged or recognized in a matter-of-fact, natural way; or responded to negatively, such as with ridicule, can contribute significantly to the willingness and enthusiasm with which students respond to the teacher or ask for help in their learning. This affect has much to do with the classroom climate for learning. Because of this, the different ways in which teachers responded affectively to students were recorded.

Observed percentages of classroom time teachers spent engaging in these various responses are shown in Table 3.4. Overall, the affective response of teachers to students was more often neutral than positive or negative. Elementary students were clearly not treated by teachers in a negative or punitive way, but neither were they praised or treated with warmth or any other positive affect with any frequency. Students lived in a classroom instructional environment rather devoid of affect.

Another important way in which teachers respond to students is by correcting their learning to be sure that it proceeds in the desired fashion. This can be done with or without guidance. That is, students can be told simply that their response is right or wrong; or they can be told that their response is right and why it is right or that it is wrong, why it is wrong, and what it should have been; or they can be helped to figure out the answer for themselves. As shown in Table 3.4, correcting responses accounted for only a small percentage of total instructional time, and students received feedback as to the correctness of their responses much more often than they were either given information about why their responses were accurate or inaccurate or helped in getting the right answer. In general, learning would have been more clearly directed by teachers if the findings had been reversed.

Discussing

A fifth major category of instructional techniques used by teachers is discussion, which is, like questioning, an important means of getting students to reveal how well they are learning. The snapshot data presented in Table 3.4 show that students and teachers were actively engaged in discussions of what was being learned less than 10% of the total instructional time.

Attending to Routines

The final category of instructional technique that observers recorded was attending to the routines that facilitated learning. It is not considered an instructional technique as such, but it is a category of behaviors in which teachers engage in order to organize for and encourage learning to proceed. Based on FMI estimates, teachers spent about one-fifth of the classroom time available engaged in getting supplies distributed, books opened, work sheets passed out, and students into work groups (see Table 3.4).

Observers in the classroom also noted snapshot estimates of how much time teachers spent getting ready for learning. Two categories of observations accounted for this expenditure of time. The first was an estimate of time spent on routines, but the focus here was slightly different than from the estimate derived from the FMI data, as just discussed. For the snapshot estimate, the observers focused on the teacher or aide and recorded only adult time spent on this activity, not the interaction between students and teachers, as in the FMI. It included such behaviors as distributing materials, arranging the furniture, taking attendance, cleaning up, or consulting with other adults. The snapshot data for these routines accounted for about half the FMI estimate in both the early and upper elementary grades (see Table 3.4).

The other category of routines for which observers were asked to record data focused on whether the teacher and students were getting ready for instruction, changing activities, cleaning up, or preparing to leave. These data were similar for both early and upper elementary grades and again accounted for about half of the FMI reports of time spent on routines (see Table 3.4). Combining the two categories, routines and preparation for assignments, thus yields figures that are remarkably similar to the FMI data — approximately 20% in all cases.

The congruence of these reports suggests that it is accurate to say that about one-fifth of classroom time was spent on routines. Time spent on getting ready for instruction, of course, is not available for learning, and whether it serves other worthwhile purposes — such as socializing students into schooling and helping to establish the climate of the classroom — is not clear from our data. From an instructional perspective at least, the rather large amount of time spent in the routines of classroom living should be closely examined. If elementary teachers in this sample could have been more efficient in preparing for activities, in changing from one to another, and in dismissing students, more time would have been freed for instruction.

Active Versus Passive Engagement

Another finding about the estimates of time centered upon how often students engaged in the more active pursuits such as discussing and responding rather than in the more passive activities such as listening to the teacher lecture or explain something. Of the first five categories of instructional practices we have been discussing, the latter four would engage students more actively in the processes of learning than would the first one (the teacher lecturing or explaining). The latter four categories of teacher behavior (and thus, by implication, categories of what students were doing) were observing and monitoring learning, questioning, responding, and discussing. The total amount of estimated instructional time for these four categories was about 50% for both the early and upper grades. For about half of their classroom time, then, students were engaged in these types of activities, while for approximately 25% of their time they were engaged in listening to the teacher lecture or explain. Listening, of course, can be an active skill, but for young children, it must be in short segments and not over used. With too much talk, attention wavers and minds begin to wander. Although it is undoubtedly necessary that students listen to their teacher for some purposes, it is desirable to have your students actively involved in their learning for as much of the classroom time as possible.

Deciding What Is Desirable for Your School

The percentages of time used for various instructional practices that you think are desirable for your school should be a topic of serious faculty deliberation. Clearly there are no absolutes of how time should be spent on each of the instructional practices. Value judgments about the importance of the learning outcomes desired and research evidence about how students learn best must be considered when you are deciding what the appropriate proportions of time are for the various teaching techniques in your classrooms.

The use of time in relation to the types of instructional practices in classrooms is one of the most basic curriculum factors which will determine what students will learn in your school. How your teachers structure learning through various instructional practices and for different percentages of time, therefore, is a fundamental classroom curriculum decision. With the recent research on how time and specific instructional practices are related to achievement (e.g., Denham & Lieberman, 1980), your faculty should be very aware of the importance of how teachers and students spend their time and the types of instructional practices that foster different types of learning.

In the hope of promoting education that is more congruent with the ideals we express, I offer here, as I have done throughout this chapter, some value judgments regarding how often teachers use certain classroom practices. Surely it is better for students to be actively involved in their learning rather than passively watching or listening to what is happening during instruction. Who would not agree that more time should be spent on instruction than on managing routines in the classroom? The amount of time spent on open-ended questions was far too limited for what I think is important in instruction. In addition, I would prefer a more positive affect throughout the classroom interactions than the neutral one our observers found. These concerns regarding the kinds of instructional practices used in your school, the proportion of total instructional time allocated to them, and their effectiveness for the types of learning you desire ought to be addressed by your faculty.

However, for your faculty to be able to decide whether classroom practices are good or bad, they must understand how practices relate to the functions and goals of the curriculum. Classroom practices in your school are only good or bad as they foster the desired learning with no undesirable side effects. As you examine the instructional practices in your classrooms, you should help teachers match them with the goals and objectives they are trying to accomplish. Only then can you determine whether they are of the type they ought to be and if they are being used frequently enough to achieve what is desired.

When the classroom practices we have discussed in this chapter are matched with the desired goals and functions discussed in the preceding chapter, we can begin to make more informed judgments about the desirability of the practices observed and reported for this group of schools. If a store of knowledge related to the different subject areas was desired as part of the intellectual function, the teachers in this sample were probably on the right track by lecturing in a neutral environment using directed questions in interacting with the students. If the basic skills in reading/language arts and math were the major thrusts of the curriculum, as has been indicated by a variety of data, then teachers were probably correct in spending good amounts of time asking direct questions, explaining the skills needed, and monitoring the work of students in acquiring them.

But there were other types of desired learning, such as those that foster social development. These include appreciation for the diversity in humankind, ability to handle conflict and achieve consensus, and attitudes toward the preservation of the environment to name a few. In order to promote this learning, classroom time needs to be proportioned more in favor of instructional techniques and learning activities devoted to open-ended questions, student-initiated interactions, and a sense of trust developed through a positive affect in the classroom. Similarly, if students are to have the opportunity to explore what is important to them, develop creativity, and attain other goals relating to their personal development, then much more student-initiated interactions with the teacher need to be present in classroom practices.

It is the knowledge of what you are trying to accomplish in the classroom — your intended curriculum — that allows you to say with certainty whether the right types of instructional practices are being used and with the right frequency. These judgments and your efforts to bring them about in practice can be very influential in curriculum improvement.

USE OF LEARNING PRINCIPLES

The use of the instructional techniques just discussed is basic to your teachers' professional skills. When using the techniques, your teachers should be guided by certain basic psychological principles. They should, for example, clearly delineate and communicate the learning task, provide feedback to students about their learning, and organize the classroom to facilitate learning. The effective use of these psychological learning principles is positively related to student achievement (Denham & Lieberman, 1980); thus, you should expect to see considerable use of them in your classrooms. This section discusses how the elementary teachers in our sample used these basic learning principles. In addition, although they are not psychological principles per se, teacher enthusiasm, behavioral objectives, and individualization are also included because of their importance to instruction.

Clarity of the Learning Task

Students in the early and upper elementary grades were asked to respond to questionnaire items about how well teachers were communicating the learning tasks to them. Early elementary students were asked to respond (yes, no, or sometimes) as to whether or not they understood what their teacher wanted them to do in their class. The results, shown in Table 3.5, suggest that, while a majority of the students said that yes, they did understand, and very few felt they never understood what their teachers wanted, a rather large percentage (40%) only sometimes understood what their teachers wanted of them. Upper elementary students responded with "usually true" or "usually false" as to whether their teacher gave clear directions. Again, although most students said their teachers usually gave clear directions, about one-fifth of the upper elementary students did not think their teachers usually gave clear directions (see Table 3.5).

These figures are a cause for concern: The percentage of students who at least sometimes did not understand their teachers was too high at both of the elementary levels. Learning does not proceed easily under such conditions. Since your teachers will generally determine the learning tasks, it is their obligation to communicate clearly to students what is to be done. Your students must understand the learning task, or they will be unable to achieve efficiently and effectively what is expected of them.

Feedback to Students

Another learning principle that educational psychologists have shown is related to some types of achievement is knowledge of results. If students are to proceed effectively in their learning processes, they must know whether what they are doing is correct or incorrect and, if incor-

Table 3.5 Use of Learning Principles, as Assessed by Student Perceptions

Learning Principle or Facilitator	Lower Elementary			Upper Elementary	
	Yes (%)	Sometimes (%)	No (%)	Usually True (%)	Usually False (%)
Clarity of Task[a]	57	40	3	80	20
Feedback	50	32	18	83	17
Organization--Students:					
Don't know task				55	45
Don't know reason for task				38	62
Teacher enthusiasm				76	24

Source: J. Wright, 1980a

[a]Lower elementary students responded to the statement, "I understand what my teacher wants me to do in class." Upper elementary students responded to the statement, "Our teacher gives clear directions."

rect, why. All elementary students were asked to respond to an item on the questionnaire that said, "If I do my work wrong, my teacher helps me to do it right." Half of the early elementary students said yes to this item, about one-third said sometimes, and less than one-fifth said no (see Table 3.5). At first glance these figures may seem acceptable, but their true meaning is in fact not very reassuring: About half of the students in the early grades indicated that the teacher did not, or at least not consistently, help them correct their work if they did it incorrectly.

As shown in Table 3.5, a much larger percentage of the upper elementary students said that the teacher usually gave feedback. However, nearly a fifth of them responded that the statement was usually false, meaning that their teacher did not help them correct their work. Although this is a relatively small percentage, it is nearly identical to the proportion of early elementary students who responded no to the same question. Taken together, these data suggest that there are too many students at all elementary grade levels whose teachers are not facilitating the learning process by helping with necessary corrections. This finding takes on even greater importance when it is recalled that another third of the early elementary students did not believe they *consistently* received important feedback from the teacher. Learning will not proceed effectively if students do not receive help from the teacher in correcting their errors.

Organization for Learning

Only upper elementary students were asked to respond to two items that related to the organization of the classroom to maximize learning. They responded with "usually true" or "usually false" as to whether they thought many students did not know what they were supposed to do and whether students had to do things without knowing why.

Slightly over half of the students said it was usually true that "many students don't know what they're supposed to be doing during class" (see Table 3.5). Nearly half of the students thought it was usually false. A large percentage, then, clearly saw their classmates as confused over what they were to do.

On the other item, slightly more than one-third of the upper elementary students thought it was usually true that "we've had to learn things without knowing why." A little less than two-thirds, then, thought their classmates knew why they had to learn things. It is interesting to note that the majority of students did not know *what* they were supposed to learn, and yet they knew *why* they were to learn it. Perhaps the explanation for this is that most students knew they were supposed to learn something because the teacher told them to.

Our data thus show that there were many students in these upper elementary classrooms who thought their teachers made their learning tasks clear and that they and their classmates understood what they were to do and why they were expected to do it. For these students, instruction seemed to make sense, and so learning for them would have been likely to occur. For far too many students, however, this was not the case. These findings should demand close attention from teachers if instruction is to be more effectively presented to all students.

Teacher Enthusiasm

Another variable linked to student learning is teacher enthusiasm. Although it is not a psychological principle, as are the three preceding items, which have been demonstrated through research to increase learning, the amount of enthusiasm a teacher shows for learning can clearly affect and motivate the students in the class. It is also an important element in the affective climate of the classroom.

Only upper elementary students were asked to respond to an item about teacher enthusiasm. They responded with "usually true" or "usually false" to the statement, "Our teacher has fun teaching this class." Over three-fourths of them (Table 3.5) said it was usually true that their teacher had fun teaching the class. Considerably more students perceived their teachers as enthusiastic than as following some of the commonly accepted psychological principles, as just discussed above. It is surprising, however, that the degree of teacher enthusiasm that the students perceived did not raise the observers' ratings of the positive affect of the classroom to a larger extent (see the earlier section on "Responses to Students").

Behavioral Objectives

Another concept that teachers have been encouraged and even required to use in order to maximize learning is behavioral objectives. The rationale behind the use of behavioral objectives is that when students are clearly told what is to be learned — that is, how their behavior is to change — learning is significantly focused and facilitated. Behavioral objectives have not been completely accepted, however, and are the subject of considerable controversy. Although the expectation that teachers will use them is widely shared by funding agencies, governmental agencies, some lay citizens, and many administrators, some educators are adamantly opposed to them (e.g., Zahorik, 1976). Others cite the limitations which the use of behavioral objectives place upon the learning process and its outcomes (e.g., Eisner, 1985; Raths, 1971). Nonetheless, the concept of behavioral objectives is compatible with the previously discussed learning principles and is also widely advocated. The teachers in the Study of Schooling sample were therefore asked to respond to a series of items about whether they used behavioral objectives and if they found them useful.

Overall, the elementary teachers responded to the use of behavioral objectives in a slightly favorable manner (Tye, 1979d). They tended to respond with "mildly disagree" to statements that were negatively worded about objectives. They mildly disagreed that objectives should not be determined in advance, were difficult to use, did not reflect what they were trying to do, were too hard to write, were too simplistic to be of value, and could be used by others to evaluate them unfairly, and that keeping records of student attainment of objectives was too time consuming. At the same time, they mildly agreed with statements that were positively worded: objectives assisted teachers in evaluating student progress, were built into instructional programs used, helped students know what was expected of them, helped teachers know what and how to teach, were more appropriate for some subjects than others, and helped evaluate their teaching.

The only exception to this trend of mild support for behavioral objectives was that many teachers mildly agreed that behavioral objectives took too much time to prepare. Due to the number of subjects an elementary teacher must teach, it is not surprising that there was a desire not to consume time in preparing behavioral objectives. Eisner (1985) made this point very vividly by estimating that, with extensive use, elementary school teachers would have to deal with 840 objectives over the course of a year. Few teachers would be supportive of such a demand.

A final question about behavioral objectives was the extent to which the teachers used instructional objectives in each of the six subject areas studied. In four of the subjects — reading/language arts, math, social studies, and physical education — elementary teachers in general reported they used instructional objectives "often." In science and the arts, they reported using objectives "not very often" (Tye, 1979d, 1979g).

This grouping is a rather curious one. Not unexpectedly, in the subjects always included as a part of "the basics" (reading/language arts and math), teachers said objectives were used often. The programs and materials used in these areas are even likely to have instructional objectives built in as an essential part. Perhaps too, the teachers were clearer about what to teach in the four subject areas they named and less clear for science and the arts.

It is also possible that, since the arts are in part an expressive, creative subject, the teachers did not see behavioral objectives as appropriate. When students are expected to express their creativity, behavioral objectives may not be a desirable concept. Less clear, though, is why science was perceived as an inappropriate subject for objectives. Perhaps it is related to another finding from our data, which suggested that science was not taught often by many teachers. It would be interesting to know more about why the teachers reported this distinction among subjects in the use of behavioral objectives.

Since the concept of behavioral objectives is a controversial one, you may want to explore the extent to which your teachers support them and use them, and the utility they think objectives have in the learning process. Strong arguments are made for them by educational psychologists, but others cite disadvantages and offer options to them (Eisner, 1985; Zahorik, 1976). Our teachers saw them as mildly useful for some subjects but not for others. It would be instructive for your teachers to discuss whether they are supportive of behavioral objectives and why and when. Such a discussion could do much to help clarify instructional decision making for your teachers.

Individualization

A final concept we studied which is related to maximizing instruction and making it more meaningful is individualization. Teachers are always exhorted to tailor instruction to the needs and abilities of their students, but as indicated in chapter 2, our teachers were given little help in doing it from curriculum guides and, seemingly, from curriculum consultants. There are many ways that teachers can individualize for students, and our teachers were asked to indicate their use of variations in seven different areas: objectives, content, methods, materials, grouping, time, and activities.

Teachers were asked to indicate how often they used variations in each of the seven areas as a way of individualizing their instruction. Two-thirds or more of the teachers reported that they individualized on each of the elements. Overall, the teachers responded that they used two methods "often": different grouping arrangements and different instructional methods (Tye, 1979c). It should be noted that these two ways will individualize *how* students learn but not *what* they learn. Less often, but still to a good extent, the teachers used variations in the remaining five areas.

This evidence suggests that the teachers perceived themselves as individualizing instruction primarily in *how* they helped students learn, not in *what* they helped them learn. They did this even though they received little help in doing so from traditional sources such as curriculum guides and consultants. We will see a real conflict in later evidence, however, between these teachers' perceptions of their efforts to individualize instruction and data from the observers about grouping patterns and activities. It will become apparent that, although teachers reported they were using several curriculum elements to individualize their instruction, observers did not perceive this.

A basic dilemma faced by teachers in their ability to individualize effectively is the need for data that can be used as the basis for their decisions. Deciding who needs individual attention and of what kind needs to be done with some factual support. We asked about the kinds of information teachers used in making these decisions. Seven different areas of potential information were identified, and our teachers were asked to respond as to how frequently they used each of the potential sources, if and when they individualized instruction for students.

Most teachers reported they "almost always" (70.3%) used their own observations of student performance and behavior and that they "almost always" (68.9%) used their own analyses of student classwork to guide them when they individualized instruction. Most teachers "often" used grade-level expectations, diagnostic test results, and knowledge of student preferences (Tye, 1979b). On the other hand, they did "not use very often" aptitude test results or student performance and behavior in previous classes. These teachers, then, reported using their own observations and assessments rather than somewhat more objective data such as test scores or grade-level expectations as bases for individualizing instruction. Diagnostic test results were used "often" perhaps because, by definition, they are designed for the specific purpose of individualizing instruction and are readily available in reading/language arts and math, the two subject areas that figured most prominently in the curriculum. Perhaps teachers would have responded that diagnostic tests were used even more often, had they been available in all subject areas.

Your faculty could productively consider the ways in which the curriculum at your school could be individualized using the seven elements we studied. Teachers should be encouraged to discuss successful ways they have found and problems they still are encountering as they attempt to individualize their curriculum. Combined with these discussions, the topic of personalization of the curriculum, as examined in chapter 2, could also be explored. Through these sessions it should be possible for your teachers to become more skillful in individualizing and personalizing the curriculum, when they consider it to be feasible and desirable. Where they are having difficulties, staff development programs could be planned, perhaps even using curriculum consultants from your district office.

TYPES OF CLASSROOM ACTIVITIES

Another factor that is very influential over what students learn while they are in school is the types of activities in which they engage. Students will learn different skills and ideas from discussion than they will from role playing, for example. Different types of activities are important in learning very different things and achieving different outcomes. In fact, Eisner (1985) calls learning activities *the* most important curriculum decision teachers can make. As such, discussions with your teachers on the types of learning activities they offer to students will be an important avenue for improving the curriculum at your school.

We collected a variety of data regarding the types of activities used in the classroom. Teachers, students, and observers all reported data about the major activities of the classroom, but not all the same activities were responded to by the three groups. Some observation data about activities have already been reported elsewhere and will be mentioned here again as appropriate, along with new data from observers. The student data were limited only to the upper elementary grades.

Upper elementary students were simply asked whether or not they engaged in several specific activities but were not questioned on the frequency of the activities. Elementary teachers were asked with what frequency their students engaged in the activities of listening to or watching the teacher, listening to other students, using audiovisual materials, reading, writing, engaging in psychomotor or physical activities, acting or role playing, and taking tests. Each of these activities will be discussed.

Listening to the Teacher

Over 90% of the upper elementary students said they engaged in the activity of listening to or watching the teacher in all subject areas (see Table 3.6). Most teachers also reported that their students engaged in this activity for all the subject areas "often," with the same order

of distribution over subject areas as shown in the student responses
(J. Wright, 1980a).

Listening to the teachers was a frequent activity, as indicated by
these data and by the data reported earlier on the observed use of time,
where it was found that about 25% of instructional time was spent on
explaining, lecturing, or demonstrating to students (see Table 3.4). This
conclusion was further supported by the probability computed from the
snapshot data that, for about 20% of the time, students were listening to
or watching the teachers. Thus, listening to the teacher was a fundamental learning activity in our classrooms.

Listening to Other Students

Not only did the students listen to the teacher, they also listened to
their peers as they recited and answered questions. Over half of the
upper elementary students in each of the subject areas reported that
they spent time engaged in that activity (see Table 3.6). There was a
much wider range of percentages reported across the subject areas,
however: Three-quarters of the students said they listened to classmates
during reading/language arts, whereas only slightly more than half said
they did so in math.

Using Audiovisual Materials

Another activity teachers are encouraged to offer students is the use
of audiovisual (A-V) materials. Not only does the use of A-V materials
break the monotony of reading books and listening to the teacher and

Table 3.6 Percentage of Upper Elementary Students Acknowledging Some
Allocation of Time for a Classroom Activity, by Subject Area

| | % of Students Acknowledging, by Subject Area | | | | |
	Reading/ Language Arts	Social Studies	Math	Science	Arts
Listening					
To teacher	94	94	94	91	93
To other students	75	71	55	67	n.a.
A-V Material					
TV	80	72	78	71	71
Films/slides	86	82	73	81	70
Records/tapes	80	70	65	69	73
Writing	89	88	87	82	73
Test taking	87	86	87	79	74

Source: J. Wright, 1980a

other students, but it also is uniquely helpful in teaching students certain skills and concepts. Teachers know that the availability of A-V materials is never a problem, as is evidenced by the many catalogs and visits from publishers eager to sell them their products. But were they used in our classrooms?

Teachers and students were asked to respond by subject area to three specific types of activities using popular A-V materials: (1) watching television; (2) watching films, filmstrips, and slides; and (3) listening to records and tapes. (Television was not included for the arts.) Overall, teachers did not report using any of these "most of the time" and only used tapes and records in reading/language arts and the arts. Only in social studies and science were films, filmstrips, and slides used with any frequency, that is, "often."

Of particular interest was the finding that television was not used often in any of the five subject areas and, in fact, in math, teachers reported they "never" used it. Slides, recordings, films, and filmstrips were used somewhat sparingly and only in specific subject areas. The use of A-V materials in activities was not a frequent occurrence in most of these classrooms, according to teacher perceptions. Thus, the benefits of these materials to learning activities were typically not available for the students in our sample.

Students, however, responded in fairly large numbers that they engaged in watching and listening to filmstrips and television, although they were not asked about the frequency with which they did this in their classrooms. Overall, approximately three fourths of the students said they had experienced the use of A-V materials, including television, in their classrooms (see Table 3.6). There was a particularly wide discrepancy between how often teachers reported using television and student perceptions of the use of television (only whether it was used, not how often). Perhaps this was due to the fact that on those infrequent occasions that the teachers reported, students really remembered it. Another interesting discrepancy was that teachers reported never using TV in math; yet almost three-fourths of the students reported its use. It is difficult to explain such variation in perceptions. Data such as these should be followed up in more depth as you study your school.

Our classroom observers were asked to record information every 15 minutes about what each adult and student in the classroom was doing, size of groups, and what activities were in progress. These data are referred to as classroom snapshot (Giesen and Sirotnik, 1979). The snapshot data provided more information about the use of audiovisual materials in the classrooms, permitting an estimate of the probability of students having been engaged in listening to or watching A-V equipment. These figures (6.8% for the early elementary students, 4.9% for upper elementary students) were quite low and corroborated the teachers' reports of rather infrequent use of A-V materials. Overall, our data suggested that the infrequent use of A-V materials reported by teachers and observers might have been a memorable event in the classroom for the large numbers of students who simply reported they had engaged in those types of activities.

Reading

Reading is one of the most basic activities in which students engage while they are learning. Teachers were asked to respond to the frequency with which they had students read in three subject areas: reading/language arts, social studies, and the arts. The teachers responded that they had students read "often" in all three subject areas. Reading to learn is a frequent activity in the classroom, according to the perceptions of the elementary teachers. Upper elementary students were asked only to answer yes or no as to whether they read in their reading/language arts class. Over three-fourths (78%) of them said yes, they did read.

It is puzzling as to why an even greater percentage of students did not respond in the affirmative to this question. What did some students do in their reading class, if not read? Did reading instruction for them consist only of learning the skills involved, without ever really immersing themselves in reading? This might be a distinct possibility, and it would be in keeping with the remedial thrust of reading in the upper grades, which is discernible through the analysis of classroom materials. It is also possible, as suggested by other data, that the students focused on the follow-up activities in the reading lesson (more on this later).

The impact of this finding on the reading program should have been explored further, but we were unable to do so. You might want to examine carefully any such discrepancy in perceptions found in your reading program, as well as its impact. Do your students believe that reading is an activity they have opportunities to do daily in their classrooms? If not, what do they do in their reading class, and is that what they ought to be doing in order to learn to read? For the elementary student, learning to read is a fundamental goal and reading to learn is a fundamental activity. Whatever affects this goal and this activity must be monitored very closely for the impact on your students.

The probability of a student having been observed in reading as an activity was computed from the snapshot data. In the early elementary grades, the probability was 6% and at the upper grades it was 5.5%.

The fact that students were not likely to have been observed reading as a classroom activity is puzzling, given the strong emphasis reported earlier on reading/language arts in the curriculum. Perhaps teachers were more prone to interact with students while observers were present, rather than assign a reading activity.

Writing

Work on written assignments is another type of activity commonly associated with school work. As can be seen in Table 3.6, at the upper elementary level about three-fourths or more of the students reported they engaged in writing answers to questions in every subject area. Reading/language arts had the highest number (89%) of students who reported they engaged in this activity. In fact, more students reported that they wrote rather than read in reading/language arts, which is further evidence that they did activities other than read during reading time. This could have been the result of students focusing on the follow-up activities that are always assigned to students after a directed lesson. Perhaps, too, the writing assignments were more memorable for some reason (harder? easier? boring? interesting?) than were any reading activities which occurred. The lowest percentage for any of the subject areas was in the arts, but even there 73% reported writing assignments, which included creative writing.

The probability, based on the snapshot data, that students would have engaged in written work (28.3% for the early elementary students and 30.4% for the upper elementary students) was considerably larger than was the likelihood that they would have engaged in reading (J. Wright, 1980a). Perhaps this difference occurred because so many reading activities are often followed up by a writing activity. This may have been what our observers noted. All of our data, then, suggested that working on a written assignment was a common activity in this sample of classrooms.

Engaging in Psychomotor or Physical Activities

Involvement in psychomotor or physical activities is another possible way for students to learn. It is particularly encouraged and expected in the early years of schooling because of the desire for students to be more actively involved than they are when reading, writing, and listening. Thus, we asked observers and teachers to report data on this type of activity.

The probability that the observers would have seen students engaged in this activity was low, only 7.3% for the early grade students and 5.3% for the upper ones (J. Wright, 1980a). Contrary to the observation data, however, teachers reported they "often" had students build, draw, make things, or perform in reading/language arts, social studies, science, and the arts. Only in math did most teachers report "not very often" having students engage in physical activities. Again, we see a discrepancy in our data: Although the probability was low that observers would see psychomotor or physical activities, teachers reported that they often had students engage in them.

Acting or Role Playing

Teachers and students were asked to respond regarding the use of another more physical activity — acting or role playing. Less than half of the students in the upper grades said they acted or engaged in role playing in any of the three following subject areas: reading/language arts (49%), the arts (44%), and social studies (41%). They were not asked to report on the frequency of these opportunities, however.

Teachers reported that for reading/language arts and social studies, their students did not very often engage in acting or role playing. Similarly, the probability of an observer seeing students engaged in a simulation or role play was small: 0.2% in the early grades and 0.4% in the upper grades. From all our data it was clear that the opportunity to take on the role of being someone else, with all the benefits of that experience for social and personal learning, was quite limited for the students in this sample of elementary classrooms.

Taking Tests

Taking tests was the final activity we asked about. About three-fourths or more of the students said they took tests in the five subject areas (see Table 3.6). By contrast, teachers reported that they "never" had students take tests in the arts and that they had them take tests "not very often" in social studies and science (J. Wright, 1980a). As might be expected, however, they "often" had students take tests in reading/language arts and math.

There are discrepancies between the data we obtained from the students and the teachers regarding whether students took tests. The discrepancy is hard to explain. It may have been that students perceived some activities as tests when their teachers did not, even in the arts. Such a discrepancy is worthy of following up, should you find similar differences in how students and teachers perceive your classrooms. You should investigate the following:

- What kinds of activities do your students see as "tests"?
- How do your teachers label and structure their attempts to evaluate learning?
- What do the tests your teachers give actually ask of students?

Testing is a very important activity in most schools, and our students seemed to have gotten that message.

The probability of our observers seeing students taking tests was low: 2.2% for the early elementary students and 3.3% for the upper-level students. Again, it is possible that teachers purposely did not schedule tests when they knew observers were to be in the classrooms. These data also support the finding that tests were not often found in the sample of curriculum materials we analyzed. Testing was not a regular feature in most subject areas for our elementary classrooms, although students reported they took them in every subject area we studied.

Conclusions

In summary, the most frequent activities that the students in our sample engaged in were listening to the teacher, listening to other students, reading, doing writing assignments, and taking tests in reading/ language arts and math. The emphasis on these activities is supported further when the reading/language arts emphasis noted earlier in other data is added to the data reported here. On the other hand, our students were not likely to be engaged in the use of audiovisual equipment, in psychomotor or physical activities, or in role playing and acting.

Much of our data showed that students engaged largely in the traditional schooling activities of listening to the teacher and other students, reading, and writing, which tend to foster sedentary, passive learning. They did not often have the opportunity to become physically engaged in learning, to learn from audiovisual materials, or to dramatize what they were learning. Once again, we have data to indicate that, although the schools were expected to meet many different types of functions and goals, the practices of the classrooms did not reflect these expectations and desires. Only the intellectual function is served well by the types of learning activities we found in the classrooms, and even intellectual goals can be served well by a greater variety of learning activities. The gap between the intended curriculum and classroom practices became clearer.

Nothing is more fundamental to an improved curriculum than the types of learning activities offered to your students. What students do in your classrooms determines what they will learn. Thus, classroom practices must be closely linked to the goals and objectives of your intended curriculum. In many ways, the quality of learning activities may well be the bottom line in curriculum reform. Data you collect and interpret about the types of learning activities offered to your students and how they relate to your intended curriculum are among the most important on which you can base your decisions about curriculum improvement.

APPROPRIATENESS OF LEARNING MATERIALS AND CONTENT

A final focus on classroom practices was to examine more closely the learning materials and content the teachers used in their classrooms. It is estimated that between 90% to 98% of a student's time in the classroom is spent interacting with learning materials (Komoski, 1978), and often it is these materials that actually define the content the students ultimately learn. How appropriate the materials and content are for your students thus becomes a significant curriculum question.

Teachers in our sample were asked to estimate the percentage (in 25% increments) of students, in each of the six subject areas, for whom they felt the available materials and content were appropriate. They were asked to use three student criteria: ability level, ethnic or cultural background, and interests. Overall, the teachers estimated that the materials and content were appropriate for about 75% of their students on all three criteria.

There were differences, however, in the ways teachers rated the materials and content on the three different criteria. First, how did the materials and content match up with student ability level? Social studies and science materials were rated appropriate for the lowest percentages of students, according to their ability, but the teachers estimated materials and content in even these two subject areas were appropriate for over 50% of their students. Physical education and the arts had the highest estimates, with these materials and content rated appropriate for the ability level of over 75% of the students. This is not surprising, since few commercial learning materials or packages are used in these two subjects. Further, the actual materials used in these two subjects are often objects from students' daily environment that have considerable inherent appeal: balls, climbing equipment, crayons, paints, and so forth. Materials and content in these two subjects are very different from the texts and other printed materials usually used for the subjects we studied. Finally, reading/language arts and math materials and content were also seen as appropriate for over 75% of the students, on the ability-level factor (Tye, 1979a). In general, then, the learning materials and content used by the teachers in this sample were perceived as appropriate for the ability level of the majority of students.

The responses to the two criteria of ethnicity and interest suggested that the content and materials were not quite as appropriate in all subject areas. Again, in physical education and the arts, they were seen as appropriate for over 75% of the students on both criteria, and the same figure applied to math. Social studies, science, and reading/language arts content and materials, however, were seen as appropriate for under 75%, but still over half, of the students, on both criteria. For these latter three subject areas, interest as a criterion for appropriateness of materials accounted for slightly more students than did ethnicity.

Thus, content and materials were rated as appropriate by the teachers for at least the majority of students, on all three criteria and in all six subject areas. The arts and physical education had the largest number of students for whom the materials and content were appropriate. Math fared better than some subjects, perhaps because so much attention has been paid to developing materials on differing levels so that they would be appropriate. This also might be expected to be true of reading/language arts materials and content, but they did not fare so well on the criteria of interest and ethnicity. These materials and content would reflect ethnicity much more than math materials. Your faculty needs to examine reading materials very carefully for these two criteria especially. Social studies and science content and materials were rated on all three criteria as inappropriate for less than 50%, but over 25%, of the students.

It will be difficult to find one basic text — and the textbook is still the single most prevalent learning material in most classrooms — that will be appropriate for all of your students today. The increasing diversity of students in their ethnicity, abilities, and interests make selecting appropriate materials a particularly difficult challenge. Perhaps a decreased reliance upon the basic text and more emphasis on materials and content from your students' immediate world, as well as on paperback modular materials, would help to increase the appropriateness of materials and content for your students in most subject areas. Even though our teachers' responses show that the majority of their students are being served well, more varied materials need to be developed and they need to be selected more carefully so they will be appropriate for even larger percentages of students. Much attention has been given recently to improving the quality of learning materials, but from the estimates of this sample of teachers, the efforts to improve them must be increased. There were still too many students in the classrooms who did not have appropriate materials and content for their learning.

If your teachers rely upon a basic text or any other limited set of materials and content for students, it will be difficult for you to have appropriate content for all, or perhaps even most, students. What you might consider is a greater variety of materials in more flexible forms than basic texts, increased opportunity for students to choose what they want to study on some occasions, and materials on differing levels of difficulty for major concepts and skills. Teachers also must develop the necessary skills for evaluating materials and content for their students and the time needed to do the task. Unless your teachers receive help in the important task of selecting appropriate materials and content, some of your students may not have the kinds of materials and content they need in order to learn what you expect them to.

THE INTENDED CURRICULUM AND CLASSROOM PRACTICES

In this chapter we discussed how a sample of elementary school teachers and students responded to some of the basic and continuing considerations in curriculum development and effective classroom practices. The results may be summarized as follows:

- Time in the classrooms was largely spent on instruction.
- The curricular emphasis was predominantly on reading/language arts, with math the next most emphasized subject.
- Students were expected to spend half an hour per day on homework.
- Teachers used good instructional practices much of the time, although the use of recommended learning principles was largely restricted to certain subject areas.
- Traditional types of activities, especially those that foster passive learning, were the most prevalent.
- The learning materials and content made available to the majority of the students were appropriate.

Many specific issues for you to consider were addressed in the discussions in relation to each of these classroom practices. This section will focus on some overarching issues that are imbedded within most classroom practices in any school.

Your school may well have different data on the basic practices discussed throughout this chapter, and your teachers may engage in quite different practices from this particular sample of schools. But your teachers must — and will — deal with each of the areas of practice we discussed in this chapter in some way. They are fundamental to schooling. None of your teachers can avoid dealing with them in some manner, if they are to be successful in fostering some goals of the curriculum in their classrooms. Discussions could be held which focus very explicitly on how your teachers think classroom practices ought to be conducted and on how they really are carried out in their classrooms in relation to the goals you value. Classroom practices clearly have educational consequences, and these must be rationally and deliberately examined by your faculty as a fundamental part of your curriculum improvement efforts.

As you collect your data about classroom practices, a major issue is likely to emerge as an important one for your faculty to explore. This is the fundamental relationship between the desired functions and goals of the intended curriculum and the classroom practices of teachers. Little attention is typically given by teachers to the *variety* of classroom practices needed to implement a balanced curriculum. Instead, the emphasis has been primarily upon one aspect of teaching, about which much has been written in recent years: how time is spent in classrooms and, in the opinion of some researchers, how it ought to be spent. For example, research has indicated that academic learning time (ALT) is correlated with academic achievement (Denham & Lieberman, 1980). ALT, defined as the amount of engaged time on appropriate learning tasks for students, has become a standard of successful classrooms. As a result, administrators and teachers are exhorted to monitor and increase ALT, so that academic achievement can be increased.

This is an argument that few will take issue with; after all, who would speak against academic achievement? You surely would not want your school to neglect it. And yet, you must carefully examine the assumption that more of the type of classroom practices that foster academic achievement is always better. This has become a popular recommendation for curriculum improvement, but it is one that your faculty must consider carefully before deciding that it is something you should, indeed, do at your school. This popular recommendation may be wrong for your school, if you are attempting to offer a more balanced curriculum.

Although ALT, as it has been defined in the research literature, was not investigated directly in this study, several compatible practices were found: the dominance of the teacher, the use of behavioral objectives, the monitoring of student responses, the use of direct questioning, the use of traditional activities, clarity of instruction, feedback to students, and total-group instruction. These practices are associated with increased academic achievement. Clearly, within this sample of schools, the parents, teachers, and students gave strong support for the intellectual emphasis of schooling. Since many of the classroom practices we found are related to academic achievement, they are very appropriate for all schools with a concern for the intellectual development of their students. Your teachers should clearly be encouraged to use them — and use them even more effectively than this sample of teachers did.

But if you have support for a variety of educational emphases — a balanced curriculum, as discussed in chapter 2 — the classroom practices of your teachers should be conducted and judged based on all these desires and expectations, not just on intellectual development. Very fundamental questions must be raised of your teachers, then, about the extent to which their classroom practices relate to and support all the desired functions and goals of schooling:

- Do your teachers attend to the other three developmental areas (social, personal, and vocational), if you find considerable support for them?
- To what extent are the other desired goals encouraged by the classroom practices you document at your school?
- What classroom practices should be developed so that all the desired goals will be achieved by your students?

Your school will not meet the diverse goals that our parents, teachers, and students wanted if your teachers use only the kinds of classroom practices we found. For example, a focus on ALT and related practices is not necessarily compatible with personal development and the curriculum goals associated with it. For your students to pursue their own interests and talents, to become autonomous learners, to build knowledge of and self-confidence in their abilities, and to develop their creativity are outcomes not so easily fostered by classroom practices that are as directive and teacher controlled as ALT. Your students will need time to explore and follow their interests and ideas in ways that do not permit outcomes to be predetermined by teachers through behavioral objectives and direct instruction. The time you allocate to personal development must be much more loosely structured. Your students need time for exploration and reflection; open-ended questions must be used for which no correct answer exists; students must be in control of some part of their learning; and teachers must listen to their students and encourage them to develop and pursue their own plans for learning. Unless these alternative classroom activities and behaviors on the part of your teachers and students are used, the personal functions and associated goals of schooling that you may desire will be seriously neglected.

Similarly, social and vocational development, if they receive support at your school, will be better served by different classroom practices than those used to help students meet the intellectual and personal goals. Classroom interactions among students and a variety of adults (and interactions with people outside the classroom) must occur if your students are to learn how to interact effectively with peers and adults, to respect and value people who are different from them, to understand how our government works and why they must become involved in political actions, to resolve conflict among people, to solve problems, to be aware of how people earn a living in our country, to begin to imagine themselves as workers, and to develop the skills and knowledge they will need to join the workforce.

Opportunities must be provided for your students to become involved in and take responsibility for social and civic activities in and beyond the classroom. Your students must have opportunities to experience in positive ways a variety of cultures and to interact with different types of people on an experiential level, not just an abstract intellectual level. They will need the opportunity to engage in role play in order to appreciate alternative perceptions regarding people and complex social issues. Similarly, if they are to develop skills important to the world of work, excursions into the community must be conducted and a variety of ways in which people make a living must be explored firsthand.

These types of activities are as essential to the social and vocational emphases of schooling as reading, writing, discussing ideas, and listening to the teacher are to the intellectual emphasis. It is essential that the classroom practices of your teachers be deliberately varied if they are to help your students achieve different, but equally desirable, outcomes of schooling.

Within the sample of schools reported on here, there were serious gaps between what was desired for the school and the classroom practices of the teachers. To close the gaps would require much faculty discussion and revision of classroom practices. The large amount of time devoted to teachers talking to students and the limited amount of time allowed for students to talk to teachers and other students restricted the personal and social development of students, as did the limited time for reflection and the lack of open-ended questioning. Students' perceptions of the lack of use of important learning principles such as establishing purposes for learning, organizing the classroom for learning, and knowledge of results undoubtedly limited the maximum development of the intellect of students. The limited array of activities — which emphasized only reading, writing, listening, and taking tests in reading and math, to the exclusion of role-play and audiovisual materials — hampered social and vocational development. The passive, traditional nature of learning and the limited degree of individualization impeded the personal development of many students. Curriculum improvement will not occur until ways have been identified to close these gaps between what was desired and what was being practiced in the classrooms.

How much time is to be spent on each of the functions and related goals desired for your school becomes a value decision, which you must not make lightly. If all classroom time in your school is devoted to improving ALT, only certain outcomes of schooling will be achieved while others will be lost. Different uses of time, different activities, different grouping patterns, and different materials must be present in each classroom if outcomes related to personal, social, and vocational development are also to be attained. It will be a challenge for your faculty to set clear priorities, but the functions of schooling you value should not be eliminated from or neglected by your curriculum. All that you desire must be fostered by appropriate classroom practices.

A most serious task confronting you is to address the basic issue of how time in your classrooms should be spent and is spent — in pursuit of what ends, to what degree, and using what classroom practices to attain all the desired goals. The interaction among how time is spent in classrooms, desired functions and goals within a balanced curriculum, and the development of classroom activities appropriate for all your goals must receive your constant and conscious consideration. To bring about the desired outcomes of schooling, your teachers must plan and implement classroom activities designed expressly to do this. To have the desired outcomes out of alignment with practices is to run the risk of never achieving what is desired and to fail to educate your students properly. When desired goals are aligned with different but compatible activities and classroom practices, your students will become educated people who can function well in our complex, ever-changing society.

CHAPTER 4

Curriculum Decision Making and Attitudes

A basic issue in curriculum development is who should make curriculum decisions. Those who have power in the process have great potential control over what students will learn in school. Good arguments are made for a variety of people and groups to be involved in curriculum decision making, although opinions vary on this subject. The arena for curriculum decision making is very complex, since many people and groups want to be, and are, involved.

Although the federal government gets directly involved in curriculum decisions only periodically and just for certain kinds of programs, federal agencies have considerable power in limited areas. Usually required for federal funding are statements of goals, some possible activities, and how the project will be evaluated in order to determine its success; and these are all basic curriculum decisions. Thus, whenever funding for a program comes from the federal government, the curriculum is likely to be affected.

Primary responsibility for education lies with the states, and we are currently moving to more and more state control over the curriculum (Klein, 1987). The states have always been among the most powerful participants in curriculum decision making, through direct acts of the legislatures, departments of education, educational commissions, and other such agencies. Some states make many fundamental curriculum decisions: deciding what texts are required or recommended; selecting which tests will be given and with what frequency; establishing general aims, goals, content, and methodology through curriculum guides; creating state-mandated curriculum areas and programs; setting general standards and requirements to be met; and determining new curricular thrusts for the future.

Most local districts pride themselves on their right to maintain control over the schools and the curricula within their political boundaries. Policy advisory councils are appointed; district curriculum planning occurs; materials are purchased and developed; facilities are planned, built, and maintained; and a whole host of other decisions with impact on curriculum are made by the local district. Although the states are now taking some control away from the local districts, curriculum decision making in some aspects is still very central at this level.

Local schools are also active in curriculum planning, although some research has documented that they are the weakest link in the chain (Griffin, 1979). Faculties often, however, plan what courses will be taught, select supplementary materials, establish centers for instructional materials, agree upon standards of performance for promotion from one grade level to another, and deliberate upon the general aims and goals for the school. Much of the literature on both effective schools and the need for changes point to the importance of the local school as the crucial site for effecting change and curriculum improvement (e.g., Edmonds, 1982; Goodlad, 1975; McLaughlin & Marsh, 1978).

In chapter 2 we discussed the essential role of the teacher in curriculum decision making at the classroom level, acknowledging that the teacher is, in actuality, always a participant in the decision-making processes. Ultimately, the teacher has great power over curriculum decision making because all the other efforts are generally directed at and funneled through the classroom teacher. The teacher must not, and in practice cannot, be bypassed in curriculum decision making.

More basic, perhaps, than all other influences on curriculum decision making is that of textbook publishers. It is generally acknowledged that the textbook is an extremely powerful determinant of the curriculum. Very powerful, too, are general societal groups who have great interest in the schools and who often try to get their current concerns into the decision-making process. (For a more extensive discussion of the curriculum decision-making levels, see Goodlad, Klein, & Tye, 1979.) Clearly, curriculum decision making is a complex arena with many participants in the processes. There are few guidelines to help you make sense out of the complexities of the field and arrive at judgments about what is good and what is bad within the arena of curriculum decision making. Ultimately, what you decide ought to be happening at your school is a value judgment that is just as legitimate as the value judgments of anyone else. Different assumptions will account for different value judgments.

What we are more interested in here, however, is not who *ought* to make curriculum decisions, but the practical question of who had power over the curriculum in the sample of schools we studied and who has similar power at your school. In assessing our sample, the focus is primarily on the roles of the teachers and students. In addition to who made decisions about the curriculum, we will also examine some basic attitudes that were held about the curriculum of these schools, using the following questions:

- How satisfied were people with the curriculum being offered?
- Did the perceptions vary significantly from parents to teachers to students?
- What implications can be drawn about the curriculum, based on the reported attitudes important people held about it?

Specifically, we examine teacher and student participation in the development of curriculum guides and the amount of control teachers believed they had over curriculum decisions. Perceptions of students in regard to their opportunities to make decisions in their classrooms are also reported. Finally, data about parent satisfaction with the curriculum, teacher satisfaction with their curriculum decision making, and student perceptions of the subject areas are included.

As with the topics examined in the other chapters in this book, you are encouraged to study similar questions about curriculum decision making and attitudes toward the curriculum at your school.

INFLUENCES ON THE CURRICULUM

The literature on curriculum change emphasizes involving those who will be most directly affected by decisions made about improvements for the school. Through involvement, ownership is developed and the desired changes become clarified and internalized and thus are more likely to occur. Projected changes that come as pronouncements from on high or from the outside experts inward to the schools, with little involvement of teachers, do not fare very well in improving the schools (e.g., Goodlad et al., 1974; McLaughlin & Marsh, 1978). These conclusions point to the importance of involving teachers as significant partners in any attempt to improve the curriculum. Unless you do so, the chances are very good that you will not have a successful improvement program at the classroom level. You might arrive at a well-designed intended curriculum, but, unless your teachers are meaningfully involved, it is likely never to affect the classrooms of your school.

The following thus become important curriculum questions:

- How did our teachers perceive themselves as curriculum decision makers?
- Was the decision making shared among those who were most

directly affected, so that efforts were maximized to bring about the type of curriculum desired?
• Did students share in curriculum decision making?

In addition to reporting new data that relate to these questions, I will refer back to earlier data that will also help answer the question of who made curriculum decisions at the local school level.

In chapter 2 it became clear that several sources that were thought to be influential in curriculum decisions had a more diminished role in this sample of schools than we anticipated. Parents as well as district consultants were perceived by teachers to have low influence over what teachers planned to teach. Textbook publishers and curriculum guides had only moderate influence in most subject areas. The teachers themselves and their students were the only two sources of high influence across all subject areas.

Other evidence we have already considered is also related to the question of curriculum decision making. For example, although teachers were consistently involved in the preparation of the curriculum guides that we examined, most guides listed only one teacher, or at most a few teachers, as author. Significant numbers of teachers apparently were either never involved in the development of these guides or were not publicly recognized for their contribution (Klein, 1980a). Further, it was noted in chapter 2 that the guides assumed that teachers were curriculum users, not curriculum decision makers. The sample of guides analyzed gave little evidence of helping teachers become skilled in curriculum development processes. These data suggested that teachers were not significantly involved in this aspect of formal curriculum decision making at the state or district level, nor did they receive help from the guides in becoming skilled in making curriculum decisions in their classrooms.

Clearly, teachers perceived themselves and their students as having influence over the curriculum, although they were not involved in any significant way in the development of curriculum guides at the state and local level. This finding may help explain why curriculum guides are not more influential over classroom practices. But the more specific questions to be discussed here are

• How did teachers perceive their role in making curriculum decisions for their classrooms?
• How did their role relate to the role of students in making curriculum decisions?

Teacher Decision Making

Teachers were asked to respond to a series of questions asking about the amount of control they had, in their planning and teaching, over nine elements of the curriculum. These elements were:

1. Setting goals and objectives
2. Using classroom space
3. Scheduling time use
4. Scheduling instructional materials
5. Evaluating students
6. Selecting content, topics, and skills to be taught
7. Grouping students for instruction
8. Selecting teaching techniques
9. Selecting learning activities

Most elementary teachers responded that they had "complete" control over the last two: selecting teaching techniques and learning activities. They reported "a lot" of control over all the other elements, ranking them as follows: evaluating students; grouping students for instruction; using classroom space; setting goals and objectives; selecting content, topics, and skills to be taught; scheduling instructional materials, and scheduling the use of time (J. Wright, 1980a). In general, then, the elementary teachers perceived themselves as having rather extensive control over the nine curriculum elements in their planning and teaching.

When we add to this perception the earlier conclusion that teachers also did not perceive undue influence from potential sources of influence outside the classroom, we get a strong impression that the teachers were very much in control of curriculum decision making. Yet they received very limited help in learning how to make curriculum decisions from some potentially available sources such as curriculum guides and district consultants. Further, teacher education programs are not noted for the strength of the curriculum courses offered in preservice work. The question must be raised, then, as to how well prepared the teachers were in the skills needed to exert such extensive influence over the curriculum in effective ways. We will delay this discussion until the end of the chapter, after we have considered other data.

It is interesting to note, however, that our sample of teachers reported more influence over curriculum decision making than might be expected in these times of state influence. Much of the current literature is reflecting — and sometimes deploring — the extensive control the state now has over curriculum decision making. Although it has been advocated that control be returned to the local school (Finn, 1986; Goodlad, 1984), there is little evidence to suggest that this will occur soon. Rather, more state control would seem to be the trend for the future, not less. What is occurring must not be confused with what ought to occur, however. The role of the local school and district in curriculum development must continue to be seriously debated in an open forum, to determine the appropriate balance in decision making between these two fundamental powers.

Student Decision Making

What did students report about their involvement in making decisions about their curriculum? What opportunities did they have for making decisions about what and how they learned? When it came to making choices about the intended curriculum, they seemed to have few opportunities. Students were virtually never mentioned as contributing to the development of curriculum guides. Apparently their input into this process was never even solicited, or, if it was, the fact was never publicly acknowledged (Klein, 1980a). The intended curriculum was something designed by adults for students, not with students.

What about opportunities for students to make curriculum decisions in their classrooms? Data about curriculum decision making, comparable to those collected from teachers, were also collected from students, although not in as much depth. Students were asked some very specific questions about the degree to which they helped in making decisions about what they learned (content) and did (activities) in their classes. Over half of the elementary school students said they did not choose the activities in their classes. In response to other items that were only presented to upper elementary students, over four-fifths said they did not make decisions about the content they learned in class (J. Wright, 1980a), and over two-thirds said they would like more opportunities to choose their activities in class. These figures indicate large numbers of students who believed they had no opportunity to choose what they did in their classes or what they learned. Further, at the upper elementary level, there was strong student sentiment for having more opportunities to make decisions about how they learned.

Another question specifically asked elementary students to report on their involvement in choosing their learning materials. On average, 40% said they "never" got to choose the books, materials, and equipment used in their classes; 60% reported making such choices either "sometimes" or "whenever I want to." This indicated that, even though most students did not perceive an opportunity to make decisions about the content they learned and about half of them were not involved in decisions about the activities they engaged in, more of them said they did have at least some opportunity to choose their learning materials.

These percentages, however, are based on the total number of students across all subject areas. When the subject areas were analyzed separately, some interesting differences appeared. Nearly half the students indicated they "never" got to choose their materials in math and social studies. Choice was somewhat more available in science and in reading/language arts (somewhat over one-third responded with "never"), but only in the arts did the proportion of students who said they "never" had a chance to choose their materials drop as low as one in four.

In my judgment, these data reveal that there were too many students whose opportunities to choose materials in all their subjects were much too limited. It might be expected that the arts would provide many opportunities for students to select their materials and yet, one-fourth of them said they never had the opportunity, even in that subject. In reading, I believe there must be ample opportunities to choose books if students are expected to develop an interest in and appreciation for reading. Yet over one-third of the students in this sample reported they never had this chance. Surely students who read only materials selected by adults (probably only textbooks) are unlikely to achieve all the goals of the reading curriculum. It has been clear for many years that the books children like are not necessarily the same as the ones adults would choose for them. Further, the limitations of reading texts as the sole mode of instruction are well documented (see, for example, the articles in "A Closer Look at Textbooks," a 1985 special issue of *Educational Leadership*). Such evidence clearly suggests to me the need for all students in a comprehensive reading program to select their own materials for at least part of the time.

Similarly, the percentages of students never having the opportunity to choose their learning materials in the other three subjects of math, social studies, and science were too high. Were these subjects also only taught from a text or from teacher-selected supplementary materials? If the answer to this was "only from the textbook," and for many students it appears this was so, we must ask

- How are students' interests ever adequately met if only adult perceptions of what they would like and be interested in are recognized?

- When do students have the opportunity to study what they select?
- When do they learn to make "good" decisions for themselves?

These are the types of questions and value judgments that must be made for your school. It is not enough to find out whether your students have opportunities to make decisions; you must also decide whether what you find out is reflective of what you want to occur.

Fundamental questions regarding whether your students have opportunities to select their own learning materials, what they learn, or what they do in their classes include the following:

- What impact will a lack of opportunity have on students' interest and commitment to schooling over the years?
- How much freedom should your students have to decide for themselves about some aspects, at least, of the learning process?
- When do they learn how to learn so that they can become skillful, lifelong learners?

How to pursue a topic of interest by locating relevant materials, selecting the information appropriate to the topic, and organizing a variety of sources is an essential skill that students must learn. It will not be learned if these decisions are consistently made for them by their teachers. Too few students in our sample had opportunities to learn such essential skills.

Thus it could be said that curriculum was something "planned for" and "done to" the students in these elementary schools. Teachers perceived themselves as having significant control over the curriculum they offered to students, but little of that control was shared with students. Few serious thinkers about the schools would advocate complete abdication of teacher control over some of the aspects of curriculum at the elementary level. Only the most radical free schools during the 1960s ever practiced this. But surely, students in the elementary school should have the right to make some choices about their curriculum. Unless they do, some important educational goals will never be achieved, and perhaps the power of the schools to keep students in attendance over time will be severely diminished.

What curriculum decisions your students should be able to make could be a serious topic of deliberation at your school. If your students have such limited opportunity to make choices, will they ever learn to make decisions wisely? Within a comprehensive curriculum, some opportunities can and must be found to provide your students with choices they can legitimately make. Doing so can only enhance the relevance of the curriculum to their interests and lives outside of school and thus reduce the gap between life inside and outside of school.

ATTITUDES TOWARD THE CURRICULUM

One of the most important factors related to the effectiveness of any curriculum is the basic attitudes regarding it. How do students, teachers, and parents react to it? Do they support it? Like it? What other feelings do they have? Dissatisfaction with and lack of support for a curriculum is a very serious handicap for any school. An intended curriculum can be relevant, current, powerful, carefully planned, and well organized, but if the teachers do not like it, are not enthusiastic about it, or do not support it, little impact will be felt by the students. Teachers may simply refuse to implement it in their classroom curricular practices, but, even if they do offer it, their lack of support and enthusiasm may communicate to students that it must not be very important. As a result, students may be reluctant to engage themselves in it, thus insuring that it remains an intended curriculum instead of ever becoming a reality in the classroom.

The question of attitudes about the curriculum thus becomes fundamental and crucial to your curriculum improvement plan.

Potential Problem Areas

Our sample was asked a variety of questions about attitudes toward the curriculum. Parents and teachers were asked to rate a list of potential problems according to whether they perceived each to be a major or minor problem or no problem at their school. The items included poor teachers and teaching, poor curriculum, inadequate resources, lack of student interest, lack of staff interest, and lack of parent interest, all of which reflect an attitude toward some aspect of the curriculum.

For both teachers and parents, each of these potentially difficult areas was perceived to be a minor problem. Neither teachers nor parents saw them as being no problem at all, but neither did they perceive them to be major problems (Overman, 1980b). As minor problems, however, each would warrant further investigation as to how the difficulties might be addressed.

We were unable to follow these up in any detail, but you might want to determine why such attitudes as you might discover about the curriculum at your school exist and how any perceived major or minor problems could be alleviated and eventually even become major assets of the school. You could hold dialogues with your parents, teachers, and students to determine what is desired — what functions of schooling are important to them, how well they are being met, and what resources are available and needed to do what is expected. Such exchanges are essential in identifying and addressing perceived problems of your curriculum. Once identified, they must be corrected to the degree possible before your curriculum will be perceived as a strength of your school.

Parental Satisfaction

Parents were more specifically asked to indicate their degree of satisfaction with the six subject areas included in the study: the arts, mathematics, physical education, reading/language arts, science, and social studies. For each of the subject areas, over three-fourths of the parents indicated they were satisfied. The lowest percentage (80%) indicated satisfaction with the arts program, and the highest percentages indicated satisfaction with reading/language arts (91%), math (91%), and social studies (90%). In the middle range was science (88%), with physical education (81%) being toward the bottom of the range (J. Wright, 1980b). These high percentages of parents who reported satisfaction with each of the curriculum areas further indicated that the parents, at least, had quite positive attitudes toward the curriculum offered to their children. Even so, the curriculum was still perceived by parents as a minor problem for some reason. They seemed to believe there was still room for improvement. This is an area for which you might want to conduct a serious further investigation should your school have similar findings.

Teacher Satisfaction

Teachers were also asked to rate their satisfaction with the nine curricular elements discussed previously in reference to the teachers' perceived degree of control. The teachers were at least "mildly satisfied" in all of these curricular areas, and in two areas — selecting content and selecting teaching technique — over half (54% and 51%, respectively) reported they were "very satisfied" (Tye, 1979h).

Teachers, then, perceived the curriculum as a minor problem, but at the same time reported mild satisfaction with the curricular elements by which they planned and taught and over which they had considerable control. Although the curriculum was not perceived as a great strength of the school and their classrooms, neither was it perceived to be in drastic need of attention and improvement. It is interesting, and will be reassuring to many educators, that this sample of teachers reported complete control and great satisfaction with the one element we might expect them to have great influence over in their classrooms: how they taught. Unless your teachers, however, perceive the curriculum to be a major source of strength, channels for communication among the faculty should be established so that your teachers can study and improve all their curricular practices until the overall satisfaction is high regarding the curriculum.

Student Satisfaction

Students at both the early and upper elementary levels were asked several questions regarding their attitudes toward the different subject areas of the curriculum. Because of the age difference, the questions asked of the two groups varied in their complexity.

Early elementary students were simply asked whether they liked the different subjects, and they responded with either yes or no. Then they were asked whether the subjects were "easy," "just right," or "hard" for them. The percentages of students who said they liked the various subject areas were consistently high (see Table 4.1). Even math and social studies, which had the lowest percentages of yes responses, were liked by about three-fourths of the students.

All subjects except math and social studies were rated as "easy" by more than half the students, and even those two exceptions were considered easy by only slightly less than half (see Table 4.1). Fewer students responded that their subjects were "just right," but combining the percentages for "easy" and "just right" reveals that 80% to 95% of the early elementary students believed that their subjects posed no real difficulties for them. Most early elementary students, then, responded favorably to the subjects in their curriculum. They liked them and found them to be at a reasonable level of difficulty, or even easy.

Upper elementary students were asked three questions about the subjects in their curriculum (music and art were included as one subject area here, called the arts). In each of the six subject areas, students were asked for responses on how much they liked the subject, how important they thought it was, and how difficult they felt it was (see Table 4.1). The students indicated that they liked the arts the most and, in fact, rated them overall as "liked very much." Social studies was liked the least, but still "liked somewhat." All the other subjects were also "liked somewhat."

This ranking of subjects by upper elementary students reflected that of the early elementary students in general, but with one important exception: Reading/language arts dropped from third place (out of sev-

Table 4.1 Student Satisfaction by Subject Area

	Art	PE	Reading/ Lang. Arts	Music	Science	Math	Social Studies
Early Elementary							
Likes subject (%)	94.5	92.7	86.1	83.8	80.6	76.1	73.6
Subject easy (%)	68.2	67.1	51.3	61.4	52.6	46.1	44.9
Subject just right (%)	26.4	28.2	38.2	29.7	34.2	36.1	34.4
Upper Elementary							
Likes subject[a]	3.7[b]	3.5	3.2	[b]	3.3	3.3	2.8
Subject interesting[a]	3.6[b]	3.5	3.1	[b]	3.2	3.3	2.9
Subject easy (%)	78.6[b]	67.1	46.3	[b]	54.5	55.0	47.1
Subject just right (%)	18.0[b]	22.6	43.0	[b]	31.0	27.3	33.0

Source: J. Wright, 1980b

[a]Data given are mean scores from a 4-point scale (1 = dislike very much/very boring; 4 = like very much/very interesting).

[b]Art and music were a combined "The Arts" category at the upper elementary level.

en) to fifth place (out of six) in the students' estimation. We can only speculate as to why this occurred, but there were some clues as to a possible explanation. The analysis of curriculum materials reported in chapter 2 suggested that the nature of reading instruction changed between these two levels from one of a developmental nature in the early grades to remediation in the upper grades. Could this shift have been a factor? And could the limited opportunities reported by students to choose their own materials have contributed to the lower percentage who reported liking reading? As noted in the previous section, over one-third said they "never" had this opportunity. Would opportunities for students to have more decision making in reading/language arts increase their liking of it? Because of the strong emphasis on remediation noted in the materials analysis, did some students tire of instruction in this subject? Whatever the cause, the drop in the numbers of students who liked reading/language arts from the early grades to the upper grades suggested a problem in the curriculum. Success in and enjoyment of reading are goals that all schools strive to achieve, but something seemed to interfere with some students' experiencing satisfaction from reading/language arts in this sample. Overall, however, upper elementary students at least "somewhat liked" the subjects in their curriculum.

Should your faculty find such a pattern, you may want to devote efforts to finding ways to increase the numbers of students who like all the subject areas. To have even small numbers of students who dislike their curriculum and find it difficult is a challenge that your teachers must consider. It may never be possible to get all your students to like every subject area equally, but your teachers should try to make each one as relevant and attractive to your students as possible.

Students' responses to the items about how interesting they found each subject to be showed a similar pattern (see Table 4.1). Most students responded that each subject was "sort of interesting," with the exception of art, which was at the top of the scale and was rated "very interesting." Social studies, at the bottom of the list, was the only subject to be rated on the "boring" side of "sort of interesting."

It is likely that many of the factors just discussed in relation to how students liked their subject areas are pertinent to a discussion of how interesting students found their subjects. The goal of your faculty ought to be to increase the interest of the subjects wherever possible. Without an interest in subjects, your students are not likely to pursue their learning with enthusiasm and retain what they learn. If this compounds over the years, a serious problem about schooling for these disaffected students can develop. This potential problem will be addressed more fully in the last section.

Like their early elementary counterparts, many upper elementary students reported their subjects were "easy" for them (see Table 4.1). Percentages ranged from over three-quarters for the arts to slightly less than half for reading/language arts. As was true of the early elementary students, when the responses for "easy" and "just right" were combined, at least 80% of the students were included. None of the subjects appeared to give upper elementary students any serious difficulty.

Comparing all three factors, we see that the interest expressed in the subjects by the students was quite similar to their liking of a subject. Math and science reversed order in their rankings on interest and liking, but the basis for this reversal is very small. The arts and physical education were the best liked, were of most interest, and were the easiest subjects for upper elementary students, while reading/language arts and social studies were the least liked and of least interest. Social studies and math were the hardest subjects.

The data on student satisfaction are intriguing and suggest some needed discussions for curriculum improvement. Questions should be raised about why reading and social studies were at or toward the bottom of the list on all three criteria. Although the percentages were not dramatically high, they were reported to be the least liked, least interesting, and harder than the other subjects. What were students reacting to in their expression of attitudes toward these subjects? Throughout our sample, social studies had consistently more negative attitudes expressed toward it. The characteristics of the social studies curriculum should be investigated along the lines of the following questions:

- Was the content uninteresting; were the activities or materials boring?
- What content, activities, and materials would have been of greater interest to the students?
- Would increased decision making by the students make these subjects more attractive?

At the other end of the scale, students throughout the elementary school sample consistently had positive attitudes toward the arts and physical education (music for the early-level students had slightly lower scores).

- Could the reason be that in these two subjects, the so-called nonacademic subjects, the activities were very different from the traditional academic areas?
- Could it be that the more physical nature of these two subjects provided a welcome break from the more sedentary nature of the other subjects?
- Could it be that they were more inherently appealing as areas of self-expression to young children?
- If so, how could the less-liked subjects incorporate more of what has inherent attraction?

The reasons for the ranking you find should be identified in order to increase the potential appeal of each subject area to students as much as possible. Knowing why your students like or do not like subjects, why they find subjects interesting or boring, and what makes them easy or hard is at the heart of any attempt you make to improve the curriculum.

It is interesting to note that, within this sample, the arts and physical education, the two subjects liked best and found most interesting by students, ranked at the bottom of the list in parent satisfaction. By contrast, most parents were satisfied with the reading/language arts, math, and social studies curricula, while students responded less positively to these. Perhaps parents were more supportive of the academic subject areas in general because of their utilitarian nature and inherent importance to later schooling and future vocations, while the students did not value their utilitarian and future contributions, tired of them, or did not find the ways in which they were taught appealing. It would be interesting to know if parents saw the subjects they were most satisfied with as more related to the intellectual emphasis of schooling, while students saw the ones they were most satisfied with as more related to personal development (see chapter 2).

This suggests an important task for your faculty, should you find comparable attitudes. It is essential that you clearly identify how each of the subject areas could contribute most effectively to each of the various desired functions of schooling:

- What can reading/language arts contribute to the intellectual, social, personal, and vocational goals of schooling?
- Why is it important that social studies be taught?
- What does science contribute to the development of your students, and what is missed when science is not a part of your curriculum?

These represent significant questions for your faculty to explore as they examine student satisfaction with each of the subject areas.

Although the variations in attitude discussed in this section are worthy and in need of further study in order to improve the curriculum, it is clear that most students, teachers, and parents in our sample had mildly positive overall reactions to the curriculum. Perhaps this should be viewed as good news to those involved in those schools. Indeed, the news could have been much worse. And yet, the data could be interpreted to reflect acceptance of and perhaps even complacency with the status quo, more than resounding support for the curriculum. Since curriculum is the substance of schooling, it must reflect the strength of your school. The challenge would be to take these basically positive attitudes and make them even more positive.

HIGHLIGHTING THE ISSUES

The teachers in this sample perceived themselves as being very much in control of decisions about each curriculum element involved in planning and teaching, although they did not appear to be very involved in curriculum decision making beyond the classroom level. Students, on the other hand, reported generally limited opportunities to make decisions about what and how they learned. They perceived more opportunity to select materials than to make choices regarding any other curriculum element.

Our sample of elementary school parents and teachers viewed the curriculum with mild satisfaction, but at the same time as a minor problem. The students in general liked their subjects, thought they were important, and found them to be easy or about right in difficulty. Teachers reported a mild degree of satisfaction with the curriculum elements involved in their planning and teaching. Clearly, the curriculum was not a source of great frustration for most of the significant people in these schools, although, as just noted, the mild support it received should not be viewed as acceptable or as a great strength of these schools, in my opinion.

For these schools to accept the status quo regarding who makes the curricular decisions and the mildly satisfactory view of the curriculum reported would be a mistake for at least two major reasons. One is that the definition and clarification of the roles of teachers and students in curriculum decision making would not be addressed; hence, as suggested in this and the preceding chapter, the adequate preparation of teachers would remain a problem. The second important reason is the potential relationship of the curriculum to the growing problem of student dropouts in later years of schooling. In the remainder of this chapter we will discuss these two reasons why a continued emphasis on curriculum improvement is important for your school, even though there may be some degree of satisfaction with the curriculum.

Roles of Teachers and Students in Curriculum Decision Making

We might be tempted to conclude that, when the teachers expressed considerable decision-making involvement and mild satisfaction with the curriculum, they must have been doing quite a good job in their classroom curriculum. It sounds as though things were going along fairly well for these schools. In fact, it is logical to speculate that there was a strong correlation between the degree of control the teachers reported they had over the curriculum elements and the mild satisfaction they reported with the curriculum. After all, most of us feel that something we have worked hard on is bound to be good.

When the data from chapter 3 on classroom practices are put up against the data in this chapter on control and satisfaction, however, I begin to think that the satisfaction was unwarranted. Our data strongly suggested that, even though the teachers thought they had considerable control over the curriculum and were mildly satisfied with what they were doing, their daily practices showed a distressingly large gap between the curriculum goals desired and what they were doing in their classrooms. Thus, I do not believe they were doing enough to provide the variety of classroom practices necessary to implement a balanced curriculum.

The reason they were not might have been because they were unprepared for a meaningful role in curriculum development. Much more probably needs to be done in helping your teachers develop the kind of skills they need in making sound curriculum decisions, if your data are similar to ours. It is likely that your teachers desperately need help in developing the types of classroom practices that will put the intended curriculum into action. Moreover, from the looks of these data, our sample of elementary teachers needed to be somewhat jolted from their false sense of security that they were doing an adequate, if not satisfactory, job of making curriculum decisions. Provided with greater insights into the reasons for the gap between what was desired and what they actually did, they could become the creators of the means for closing that gap. They needed greater variety in the kinds of activities they offered, the teaching strategies they used, and the materials that were available. In general, they needed to learn how to develop, plan, and manage a classroom for the types of curriculum outcomes they, and others, wanted their students to achieve. Helping your teachers gain such increased insights into curriculum decision making in these aspects would be one of the most fundamental and long-lasting steps you could take toward curriculum improvement.

Your teachers are clearly the most powerful curriculum decision makers; the classroom is where the real action occurs. All your attempts to improve the curriculum must be filtered through your teachers' perceptions of their students, through their own value screens about what is important, and through their abilities to deal with the proposed changes. Your teachers do, indeed, function as curriculum makers, in spite of the efforts of writers of prescriptive curriculum guides, developers of textbooks or teacher proof materials, and state department mandates. What is needed, then, is for your teachers to develop the essential skills in curriculum development and to become knowledgeable about the options available (Klein, 1986).

It is not clear, however, how your teachers can gain the needed skills. Because the typical teacher preparation program is noticeably lacking in instruction on curriculum development, new teachers will not arrive at your school with the needed skills. The one or two courses in curriculum that are offered usually emphasize only content and teaching strategies and will hardly help teachers develop skills in all the important elements of curriculum decision making. The only other major vehicle left for attending to this fundamental need of your teachers is staff development. Little that we examined in A Study of Schooling suggested that our teachers, however, found this opportunity in the type of staff development programs they reported (see chapter 6). No program for curriculum improvement will get very far under such conditions.

It is not a simple task to educate your teachers to make good decisions about curriculum development, in order to get your carefully planned intended curriculum into practice. Even the best-laid plans go awry, perhaps never so completely as with a group of 30 or so active children. Your intended curriculum may not get implemented with a high degree of fidelity for many reasons, some within the control of your teachers and some outside of it. Your teachers must be helped to develop the skills they need to implement, as faithfully as possible, the intended curriculum, where it represents learning crucial to all students. They must also be helped to modify, augment, and supplant the intended curriculum, when it becomes desirable for their own students. They must be able to plan some unique aspects of their classroom curriculum for their particular students. They might need to know, for example, how to engage in student-teacher planning; work with varying sizes of groups; ask challenging, provocative questions; improve academic learning time; plan time for reflection by their students and time for exploring new areas for learning; meet individual differences and interests; personalize the curriculum; evaluate student progress for a variety of curriculum goals; and balance activities in the classroom to avoid boredom and fatigue.

None of your teachers should be without the resources and support necessary to developing curriculum practices appropriate to your desired goals. Where the teachers in your school will get the kind of help they need in making good curriculum decisions in their planning and teaching is a fundamental question you must address. In addition to carefully planned staff development programs, you may need to bring in consultants from a nearby university and from the county and district offices. Experienced teachers with considerable work in building curricula would also be invaluable sources of help.

It must be remembered that the teachers' role in curriculum decision making is only a part of the total picture, essential though it is. Focusing on their role as an aspect of curriculum improvement must not mask the complexity of curriculum decision making. They are not the single participants. We noted at the beginning of the chapter that many groups currently make all kinds of decisions about curriculum: legislative bodies, governmental agencies, textbook publishers, school boards, political groups, businesses, parents, directors of curriculum, curriculum censors, administrators, teachers, and, to a much more limited degree, even students. The appropriateness of these varying decisions for a specific school and group of teachers — yours — and how to orchestrate them into some coherent unity have received little attention by those who would improve schools. The most common mode of handling all these decisions by a school is simply to accept and pursue whatever is proposed by the most persuasive reformer, without examining the appropriateness of the decisions in relation to some critical factors: the current curriculum, the teachers, and the students; the wisdom and skill possessed by those advocating the decisions and those who must follow through with them; and the amount of duplication, omission, and neglect created in other aspects of the curriculum. The curriculum under these conditions will quickly become diffuse, disjointed, and incoherent to teachers and students.

Perhaps it is surprising that our sample of teachers saw themselves as having as much control over the curriculum as they did. Teachers are more often than not given some textbooks from the state and other curriculum materials from the district, and they are required by the state and district to administer tests that make very powerful judgments about their success in teaching students. The district and sometimes the state gives them a recommended or required time structure for each subject area. They are exhorted by the most recent consultant to the district to try the latest teaching technique, often with no help in understanding the relationship between the technique and the goals of the curriculum. Finally, they are pressured by parents and other lay groups to teach a great diversity of content. Yet, with all these competing demands, they are given very little help in coordinating or making sense out of all the various decisions. Little wonder that our teachers appeared to close out many of the potential influences on what they taught. To coordinate all the various curriculum decisions that get made at the different levels clearly requires more time and skill than the classroom teacher has and probably ever should be expected to have. Personnel with more time, skill, and resources than the classroom teacher must take on this task.

It is a challenge to our profession to coordinate more carefully the maze of curriculum decision makers. Who should make what decision must be determined very carefully and clarified in relation to all the other decision makers. It is clear, however, that teachers will not be left out, as they are the ultimate decision makers and must therefore be helped in understanding and capably performing their fundamental role.

Also not to be neglected is assessing the role of the student in making curricular decisions and examining the potential relationship between increased student decision making and greater satisfaction with the curriculum. Hass (1987) has called the student the major untapped resource in curriculum planning, and this seems to describe our students well. Overall, they clearly were neglected in curriculum decision making. An important topic for your school to consider is how much and where it is appropriate for students to have some decision-making power. Not all your teachers will agree on this, but some important questions for your faculty to monitor over time would be:

- Where in the curriculum can students have decision-making power that will help them become independent learners?
- How much decision-making power is appropriate at your school at the various grade levels?
- Does student satisfaction with the curriculum increase as their appropriate decision-making opportunities increase?

Certainly your students will require considerable adult guidance in their education, but they also must have opportunities to make some decisions for themselves if they are to learn how to learn and are to remain independent learners throughout their lifetime. Whatever your decision is, your students must not be overlooked in curriculum decision making. After all, they are the final measure of your efforts. They can be involved and learn or they can drop out, either mentally or physically, when they are dissatisfied with the curriculum.

Curriculum and the Dropouts

Herein lies the second major reason for a continued emphasis on curriculum development skills for teachers: the potential relationship of the quality of the curriculum to the growing dropout problem in the later years of schooling. Much of the literature currently focuses on those conditions beyond schools that may contribute to the dropout problem, such as economic necessity, teenage pregnancy, and lack of parental concern and support. More attention, however, needs to be paid to the role of the curriculum in the dropout problem. Sometimes boredom, lack of teacher interest and attention, irrelevancy of the curriculum, a repeated pattern of failure, lack of clarity about what they are to learn, and other more curriculum-oriented factors are mentioned in discussions of the dropout problem. When they are, it is noted that the problems begin early in the schooling process and become cumulative over the years.

What the data discussed in this and the preceding chapter may be pointing to is the beginning of serious problems for some of our students, which might eventually cause them to drop out of school. Even though only some students — in some cases, only a few — expressed dislike for their subjects, lack of opportunities to make important decisions for themselves, frustration with the level of difficulty, lack of understanding about the learning task, and limited help from the teacher in helping them clarify what they were to do, those students need far closer attention than the students who were more positive in their outlook on the curriculum. Although our data did not clearly indicate that the same students consistently reported these negative perceptions of the subject areas and classroom practices, it is very likely that at least some students had overlapping responses in these negative perceptions. It is very possible that these conditions could be the beginning of the dropout route for some students.

Students in your school who might respond in a similar fashion with negative perceptions of the curriculum must receive additional support and help from understanding and prepared teachers. The problems and factors causing their negative perceptions must be carefully identified, deliberately addressed, and successfully resolved before they accumulate and compound over the years. Everyone recognizes the severe limitation upon human potential and the social costs associated with students who try to resolve their problems by dropping out of school. We must be equally astute in recognizing why and where the problems begin and how we can create the kind of curriculum and classroom practices that appeal to all students and in which they can experience success, at least for the major part of their time in school. Students who see no reason for what they must do, who are not adequately helped in the learning process, who do not participate in decision making about their school experiences, who see the teacher and other students as biased against them (see chapter 5), and who do not like the subject areas that they must study are clearly students at risk. Where such students exist in any number, whether they are the majority or only a small minority, they need help from all the adults in the school, as soon as their negative perceptions are recognized. To ignore them or to minimize their confusion and negative attitudes is to add momentum to a potential dropout problem. The earliest years of the elementary school are not too early to be concerned about these students. It is, in fact, where the fundamental in-school problems can first be effectively addressed and resolved.

The improvement of the elementary school curriculum for all students should be under the control of teachers who possess the needed skills in curriculum development. Preparing such teachers is an essential part of reducing the alarming dropout rate which confronts us. The student at risk in the elementary school is the one who most needs curriculum reform and capable, skilled, caring teachers. We dare not neglect these students, no matter how few they may be.

CHAPTER 5

The School and Classroom Contexts

The traditional physical image of an elementary school classroom is an ordinary box-shaped room with one teacher and about 30 students involved in the processes of teaching and learning. When the curriculum is mentioned, it always evokes an image of the teacher and students hard at work on the learning expressly designed for students so they will become better human beings in one way or another. This is the learning discussed in previous chapters, often called the explicit curriculum (Eisner, 1985). The explicit curriculum consists of those carefully and deliberately planned objectives and implemented instruction. It is what the teacher and students work so diligently on daily in the classroom.

Within recent years, however, increasing attention has been given to what else is learned, in addition to the explicit curriculum, while the teacher and students live together daily in the school and classroom. Curriculum specialists are beginning to recognize that much more is learned than just what is deliberately focused upon, that this is also an essential part of schooling, and that sometimes it may even be longer lasting than the explicit curriculum. This is often referred to as the implicit curriculum. Because it is a neglected aspect of school improvement, it is important for you to include it in any comprehensive curriculum reform plan.

What is learned from the implicit curriculum is in addition to and different from what is so deliberately cultivated in the explicit curriculum. It often arises from the physical and social contexts of the school and classroom and is sometimes quite apart from the academic work of the classroom. Because such learning often is affective, it is not as easily monitored and usually is taught more indirectly than directly. It has been referred to as the hidden, implicit, or unstudied curriculum (Jackson, 1968; Overly, 1970; Vallance, 1973/74) and consists of attitudes, emotions, and values learned in schools apart from, and in addition to, the explicit curriculum.

The recent attention to the implicit as well as the explicit curriculum has helped focus our attention on aspects of schools and classrooms that might not otherwise receive careful consideration in curriculum improvement. Many of these aspects, in fact, are not traditionally considered to be a part of the curriculum, but they do much to teach students some powerful messages. Aspects of the implicit curriculum you might want to focus on include the following:

- What are the physical characteristics of the place where your students and teachers live and work together daily?
- What physical and human resources are provided as support for learning?
- How does schooling affect the self-concept of students?
- How do your students perceive their teachers?
- How do your students perceive each other, apart from their academic work?
- How do your students perceive their school and classroom as a place for living and learning?

These questions examine some of the potential ways messages are conveyed from the implicit curriculum. As such, they represent some of the questions you may choose to study, in addition to what you would usually expect to study about curriculum.

The contexts of school and classroom living are at least as important in the daily lives of teachers and students as are reading, math, social studies, and science. The impact of what is learned through the contexts of schooling, in fact, may be longer lasting for students than what is learned in the subject areas. This chapter examines some aspects of the physical and social contexts for our sample of elementary classrooms and will help you in determining how the contexts of your school and classrooms can affect the quality of schooling your students receive in dramatic ways. Although the explicit curriculum will be mentioned from time to time, the emphasis in this chapter is on the implicit curriculum. The specific aspects we studied that related to the implicit curriculum fall into two broad categories. The first of these is the physical context of the classroom, that is, the characteristics of space and furnishings whose combined effect influences the way that students view learning. The second category, the social context of the classroom, includes such factors as the number of adults in the classrooms, grouping patterns utilized in instruction, student/teacher interactions, student/student relationships, and the self-concept of the students. The chapter concludes with a summary of our findings, a discussion of potential messages our students might have learned from the implicit curriculum of these classrooms as examples of how you might examine the contexts at your school, and suggestions for you to consider as to how some of the traditional assumptions about schooling and classroom living and learning affect the implicit curriculum.

PHYSICAL CONTEXT

The physical appearance of your classrooms must not be minimized in its impact upon teachers, students, and the curriculum. It sets the stage for what is to be taught in the explicit curriculum and can even carry important messages to your students by being a vehicle for the implicit curriculum. As such, it was an important focus for A Study of Schooling.

Observers were asked to record some of the important aspects about the physical environment of the classrooms: the use of classroom space, type and arrangement of furniture, and aesthetic aspects. In general, the typical elementary classroom was a self-contained unit (single enclosed area) with space for about 30 students (Sirotnik, 1981). Over 80% of the classrooms observed were single rooms, and most had no auxiliary space available (J. Wright, 1980a). Desks with fixed seats or movable chairs were the general furnishings (Sirotnik, 1981), and the furniture was arranged in rows in 61% of the early elementary classrooms and 74% of those at the upper levels.

The majority of the classrooms had no learning centers available to students — learning centers existed for only 43% at the early elementary level and 35% at the upper levels (J. Wright, 1980a).

About two-thirds of the elementary classrooms showed some attempt to make the facility at least somewhat more attractive and comfortable than the typical institutional surroundings. Some had plants or unusual bulletin board displays, for example, but most had no carpeting; rugs were present in only 42% of the early elementary classrooms, and this percentage declined to 23% in the upper grades. Less than 10% of the classrooms had stuffed, comfortable furniture (J. Wright, 1980a).

This general picture of the elementary school classroom reflects what has been the traditional and predominant form of physical facilities for elementary schooling for many, many years. New architectural designs for school buildings and new concepts for use of space such as open classrooms and movable walls between classrooms were not much in evidence in this sample of schools. Four permanent walls; chairs and tables or desks as furniture, arranged in rows; little auxiliary space and only some classrooms with learning centers; and a limited attempt to make the room comfortable and attractive characterized the physical context of these elementary classrooms.

These classrooms were, then, physically sterile and unenriched places for learning. Such facilities suggested that learning was a sedentary activity and occurred in limited comfort and aesthetic appeal with restricted resources. Our interest in these data here is in the potential messages that such austere surroundings might have conveyed to the students. For example, the sterile, uninteresting classrooms were likely to communicate to students through the implicit curriculum that learning was expected to be equally uninteresting and lacking in challenge and excitement, that learning was a public activity for students to engage in as they sat in rows, that what was important in the curriculum could be learned from one teacher with a few additional resources, and that classrooms should not be expected to be attractive places to live in. In fact, the physical surroundings could even have counteracted some of the desired art curriculum regarding aesthetics which might have been a part of the explicit curriculum.

In your school, you need to consider whether the physical context of the classrooms is compatible with the development of your students in all aspects.

- What are the implicit messages that your classrooms might communicate to your students?
- Is learning an active or passive activity, interesting or boring, supported by extensive materials or restricted to a limited array?
- Are the classrooms attractive, inviting places for students to live in day after day?
- Do the messages communicated by the implicit curriculum support what you want students to learn in the explicit curriculum?
- If they do not, how can the physical contexts of your school and classrooms be modified so that they contribute positively to what your students learn in school?

These are important questions for your faculty to explore together.

SOCIAL CONTEXT

The elementary school classroom is a public setting, and most of the business of teaching and learning occurs in groups and through social interactions. These groups and the types and quality of social interactions that occur between teacher and student and among the students themselves are very important aspects of the implicit curriculum. We investigated several aspects of the social context of schooling, namely, the people available for assistance to students and the grouping patterns in the classrooms, the social interactions, and the self-concepts of the students. A discussion of each of these follows.

People and Groupings Within the Classrooms

Within the traditional physical space of the classroom, there generally was one teacher with about 28 students. Half the classrooms at the early grade levels had an aide, but at the upper grade levels only one classroom in five was so fortunate (J. Wright, 1980a).

The classrooms thus were not overly crowded and in fact had fewer students than might be expected. Fewer aides in the upper grades suggests that the expectation was that the older students were able to work more independently than the younger ones were. This assumes, of course, that students understood what they were expected to do. It was noted in chapter 3, however, that sizable numbers of students indicated some confusion about their learning tasks. With few aides to assist the teacher, there was limited opportunity for the confusion to be cleared up for these students, possibly resulting in their learning that school was not a desirable or comfortable place to be. Since the teacher in most of these elementary classrooms was the only adult available to help and guide the students for the entire day, his or her skills, knowledge, and values were powerful determinants of both the explicit and implicit curriculum for the students. What the teacher knew and valued would be taught; what he or she did not know or value would not get taught.

According to the snapshot data collected by observers, grouping in activities with a teacher or an aide was not a frequent occurrence; indeed, operating as an entire class was by far the most commonly observed pattern (see Table 5.1). Larger groups were more frequent than smaller ones at both elementary levels. Only groupings of 14 or more students approached a 20% probability of being observed, and in only one other case — groups of 7–13 at the early elementary level — did the probability rise above 10%. All groupings of less than 14 students combined had only about a 23% probability of being observed at the early elementary level, and this figure dropped to about 14% in the upper elementary grades. Clearly, the students in all classrooms were much more likely to be learning with the class as a whole and occasionally in large groups than in any other grouping pattern.

The students who actually formed the groups were not static, how-

Table 5.1 Groupings in the Classroom, with Teacher or Aide Involved
in Instruction

Grouping	Early Elementary (% probability)	Upper Elementary (% probability)
Solitary (1 student)	2.4	1.7
Small group (2-6 students)	8.1	5.6
Medium group (7-13 students)	12.1	6.5
Large group (> 14 students)	19.2	18.0
Total class	58.2	68.1

Source: J. Wright, 1980b

ever, and did change over time. Our observers noted that, within a 15-minute period, the composition of a group within the classroom was likely to have changed once. Over a 1-hour observation period, there was a mean of 4.2 different groups for the early grades and 3.6 for the upper grades (J. Wright, 1980a). Thus, although the groups' composition did change in the classroom, it was more likely to be due to splintering off from a total-class activity or movement from one large group to another than to smaller groups or independent work. Also, the probability of an observer seeing the teacher direct total-class activities was 38.7% for the early grades and 44.5% for the upper grades. This suggests not only the publicness of learning but also that very limited individualization occurred in the explicit curriculum than would have been possible through the use of smaller groups.

In such traditional classrooms it should not be surprising that observers saw little evidence of cooperative learning among students. At both levels, the probability of an observer seeing a student function within any group activity as an independent learner — as the only one responsible for his or her learning — was 40%, and working cooperatively in a group with other students, only 5% (J. Wright, 1980a).

The physical arrangements and the grouping patterns clearly fostered a teacher-directed classroom in a context of large groups (usually the whole class) and structured, impersonal, public interactions. Students had few opportunities to study in small groups, alone, or cooperatively, and had little individual attention paid to them. Further, as noted in the preceding section, it was apparent that much of their learning occurred at their desks or tables. Few classrooms had learning centers or enticing areas available for students to explore independently or work together in small groups.

This picture is likely to be very typical of many of your classrooms.

It is not unlike the picture described in other studies of elementary education (e.g., Goodlad et al., 1974; Jackson, 1968). What you need to consider carefully is the type of explicit and implicit curriculum that is likely to be offered through such physical and social groupings in the classroom.

Clearly, in the explicit curriculum, the students in our sample were all expected to learn the same things, with little or no individualization. The curriculum was a common one at all times for all students. For the student who coped adequately within such a setting, the implicit curriculum might have conveyed the message that they were quite capable at learning and could interact successfully with the important person, the teacher, who determined what was to be learned as well as the learning context.

The messages from the implicit curriculum might have been quite different, however, for those students who were not able to benefit as much from the total group experience. They had limited help available for any particular problems experienced in the explicit curriculum. Thus, if they were not clear about what was expected in the explicit curriculum, negative messages about themselves may well have been communicated to them, including doubts about their own unique potentials and talents and their capacity to learn. The students might well have learned to see themselves as not being capable of succeeding in school. Further, since learning was a large-group experience with considerable structure from the teacher, what might have been learned in the implicit curriculum was that whatever an individual student was interested in or good at did not matter at school, unless the teacher taught it.

Are these the types of messages you would want communicated to your students through the implicit curriculum? You may be quite happy with the messages the implicit curriculum offers to some students, but the physical and social structures of your classrooms may need considerable modification to insure that all of your students will get the desired positive messages from the implicit curriculum, as they are communicated via classroom context.

Social Interactions

Our students and their teachers lived and worked together in the elementary school classroom for about 6 hours a day. During this time, there were few other adults for students to interact with in any significant way. Social interactions for the students were restricted to their teacher and their peers within the classroom. These social interactions can be an important factor in the implicit curriculum as it affects the quality of life your students experience in their classrooms.

As indicated in chapter 3, the learning process occurred in a neutral climate, according to the observers; that is, it was neither punitive nor warmly supportive. These instructional interactions accounted for much of the time in the classrooms, but interactions among the students and with the teacher also occurred when the routines of the classroom were being conducted, during "off-task" times, and before and after class. These interactions might have been considered more inclusive than — or just separate from — the structured learning time, and they could also have been more influential in determining the climate of the classroom. The way in which students view the general social climate of the classroom is a powerful factor in the quality of life for them while in school; thus it is a major vehicle for the implicit curriculum. How, then, did students perceive the broader social interactions with their teachers and their peers? What might they have learned from them?

Interactions Between Teachers and Students. Both early and upper elementary students were asked to respond to items that eventually formed two different scales on teacher/student relationships: teacher concern and teacher punitiveness. Items on the teacher-concern scale for the early grades related to how the student liked the teacher and how well the student thought the teacher liked her or him. Additional items were added at the upper grades which asked the students whether the teacher made the class fun, whether the teacher was friendly, and if they would have liked a different teacher (J. Wright, 1980a).

In spite of the fact that observers perceived the classroom learning atmosphere to be neutral, students perceived their teachers as showing concern for them. Early elementary students in general responded that their teacher at least "sometimes" liked them and was friendly to them. Similarly, the upper elementary students thought it was "usually true" that their teacher listened to them, made the class fun, and was friendly; and they liked their teacher and did not wish they had a different one. Most students, then, perceived their teacher as expressing a positive concern for them.

The teacher-punitiveness scale for the early elementary students asked if they were afraid of their teacher, whether the teacher got mad when they asked questions, and if the teacher was mean to them. Additional items at the upper elementary level asked if the teacher punished them unfairly, hurt their feelings, or made fun of them. In general, the students did not perceive their teacher to be punitive. Most early elementary students did not believe their teacher was mean to them or got mad when they asked questions, nor were they afraid of their teacher. Neither did most upper elementary students believe their teacher hurt their feelings, got mad when they asked questions, made fun of them, or punished them unfairly; nor were they afraid of their teacher. Although the means of both groups were toward the low end of positive on the scale and thus showed that some students responded more negatively, in general the elementary students did not perceive their teacher to be unduly mean or punitive and, in fact, believed their teacher showed concern for them.

The students saw the social atmosphere of their classrooms in more positive terms than did the observers. Perhaps the time spent, not on directed learning but on the more informal interactions with students, was when teachers were perceived as friendlier, warmer, more open, and supportive to students and, in general, more positive than when they were directing the learning processes. If this was true, the informal social interactions of the classroom must not be minimized. It may be they were more powerful in determining the overall climate of the class-room than interactions focusing on the more direct teaching and learning processes. The warmth and concern shown by the teachers in informal interactions may have sustained the students during the more neutral and demanding interactions of academic learning, so that the overall impressions of students about their classrooms were quite positive.

Interactions Among Students. An important part of school for students is the opportunity to meet and be with friends. Students usually are actively engaged in interactions with friends and classmates at every opportunity they have throughout the day at school — sometimes even in spite of the vigilance of the teacher, who tries to keep them productively engaged in learning. The peer relationships are an important aspect of the social context of the classroom. How did the elementary students perceive these student/student relationships?

Both early and upper elementary students were asked to respond to items that clustered into a peer-esteem scale. Early elementary students were asked to respond with "no," "sometimes," or "yes" to items asking whether they thought the other students were friendly, whether they had many friends, and whether they liked the other students. Upper elementary students responded to comparable items with "usually false" or "usually true," in addition to items asking if classmates cared about them and liked them, and whether they liked working with the students in the class. In general, the students had positive feelings about their peers. These students liked their classmates and felt liked in return. Students perceived friendliness and support from their peers, as well as from their teachers.

Further statistical analysis of our data revealed a positive relationship between the two measures of peer esteem and teacher concern for the upper elementary students. That is, in those classrooms where students perceived their teachers as being concerned about them, it was more likely that they also perceived their classmates as being friendly and positive (J. Wright, 1980a). There seemed to be a positive affective climate throughout these classrooms. This was not true for the early grade levels; there was no consistent relationship among the classrooms. Perhaps the newness of the school situation had not allowed the young students to clarify and consolidate their perceptions to this extent. Or perhaps the teacher necessarily spent more time in correcting students, even in the more informal interactions, so that the very young students would become socialized into the formal, public place of the classroom. For very young students, it may have been that their relationship to the teacher as the powerful adult was more important than was their relationship to peers. In making the transition from home to school, it may take some time for these new relationships to be developed and clarified. For whatever reasons, the lack of correlation between how students perceived their teacher and the other students in the early grades would be an important area to investigate further.

In addition to the peer-esteem scale, upper elementary students responded to three single items that represented important aspects of peer relations. One item had to do with competitiveness and asked students to respond with either yes or no as to whether they felt they had to do better than other students. About half (49.2%) of the students replied that they did feel competitive in relation to their classmates. The heavily minority schools and the schools with a mixed racial student body had the highest percentages of students who felt a sense of competition (J. Wright, 1980a).

A second item asked whether students perceived cliques among their peers. The item asked whether, when small groups were formed, they believed that many students worked only with their close friends. Almost three-fourths (72%) of the students believed this was true, which gives evidence that there were student cliques in the classroom. The responses of the individual schools did not show a minority, mixed, or white racial pattern, as they did with competitiveness, however. No differentiation could be made among the schools on the student clique item.

A final item on student/student relationships asked about whether or not students yelled at each other. About half (50.7%) said this was true of their class, while about half said it was not. Thus, the classrooms reflected some degree of dissonance for a good number of students.

In general, then, students perceived that they were liked and held in esteem by their classmates. At the same time, however, for a good number of students there was some degree of competition, cliquishness, and dissonance in their classrooms. Even with these conditions, however, the overall perception of students about their teachers and their classmates was generally positive. Living in these classrooms would not seem to have been unpleasant or difficult for most of the students, although there were clearly sources of tension and some negative aspects of daily life.

Implications. The "dailyness" of classroom living highlights the pervasive influence of social relationships in the lives of students at school. Powerful messages can be learned through them. Our students received overall positive messages, but for some there were aspects of classroom living that may have been difficult: students felt their teachers or peers did not like them, there was competition for which they may or may not have been prepared, teachers may have favored other students, and friendships may have been, in general, limited and strained. Learning, then, must have occurred in a somewhat unfriendly context for some students. What you find out about the social relationships among students and between teachers and students in your classrooms will have much to say about whether your students perceive school as a friendly, desirable, comfortable place to be or as a tension-filled place where they learn negative messages about other students, teachers, and themselves. It is easier to change the explicit curriculum than this aspect of the implicit curriculum, but nothing is more fundamental for you to consider than the quality of the social relationships which your students experience in their classrooms.

Self-Concept of Students

The preceding discussion reflects the more public and socially interactive aspects of classroom life. At the same time that these relationships are developing, students are learning about themselves. These perceptions of self are more private but are still very powerful. What, then, were the perceptions the students in our sample had of themselves in relation to their lives in this kind of physical and social context?

Upper elementary students were asked to respond with "usually true" or "usually false" to three different self-concept scales, each of which was composed of several items. The scales were: general self-concept (items about how the student was liked and treated by others and about personal perceptions of oneself), self-concept in relation to peers (items about how other students reacted to oneself), and academic self-concept (items about how good one was at schoolwork). Although most students responded positively about themselves on these scales (Benham, 1979), they scored highest on academic self-concept and lowest on general self-concept. Self-concept in relation to peers was in the middle of these two. Overall, they seemed to be learning that they were reasonably capable students who had friends at school. They were worthy human beings in this place called school.

We took a closer look at possible sex differences in self-concepts as measured by these three scales, for each grade level. For the self-concept in relation to peers, there were no significant differences between the sexes at any grade level. In general, both girls and boys thought their peers perceived them favorably. On academic self-concept, there was a significant difference between males and females only at the fifth-grade level, where girls held a more positive view of how well they did at school than did boys. At the fourth-grade level, boys had a significantly higher general self-concept than girls.

Overall, then, both boys and girls tended to have a positive view of themselves in relation to their functioning at school in general, to their peers, and to their academic work. Life at school and in classrooms for the majority of upper elementary students appeared not to be associated with any strong negative perceptions of themselves, as measured by the three self-concept scales.

Early elementary students were asked to respond to only three items, which composed one self-concept scale in relation to their schoolwork. The items asked about self-perceptions in relation to being a good reader, doing the best work possible, and liking their schoolwork, to which they responded with "yes," "sometimes," or "no." Overall, these young students responded quite positively to the items about themselves.

Apparently most students in our sample had positive perceptions about themselves in relation to their ability to cope successfully at school, although they might have been even more positive. They clearly were not receiving strong negative messages about themselves through the implicit or explicit curriculum. The self-concept questions were general measures, of course, and a much more detailed look would be desirable at the classroom level. The question for your faculty to investigate is whether students are learning to perceive themselves within their classrooms as capable human beings in relation to the demands of schooling and as worthy human beings in the eyes of their peers. Where there are suggestions that negative messages may be learned by your students, the practices of the school and classrooms must be examined to determine how these might be changed.

POWER OF THE IMPLICIT CURRICULUM

The power of the implicit curriculum must never be underestimated for its impact on your students. It is an important and powerful determinant of how students learn to perceive themselves in many different aspects at school. Throughout this chapter we have identified some potential messages that the students could have received in the implicit curriculum, through the structure and contexts of their classrooms. Although there are many other aspects that might have been investigated, the choice was made to study the aspects reported on here because of their basic importance and limited resources available to us. Additional aspects of the implicit curriculum that you might want to study include

The absentee rate from schools and classrooms
The extent of vandalism
Participation in voluntary and extracurricular activities
Use of the library or instructional materials center
How rules and routines are established and reinforced
The standards communicated by the teacher
The composition of social and work groups formed, and the reasons for this
The perceptions and expectations of students by the teacher

Although each of these also plays a part in the implicit curriculum, the few aspects of the implicit curriculum selected for this study provide some insight into its great potential for student learning.

Potential Messages

One message that students might have been getting from the implicit curriculum of our schools is that individuals are not as important as the group. Much of what occurred within this sample of classrooms was a group activity. Students rarely functioned as individuals pursuing their own interests. They were instructed as part of a group, the physical arrangement of the classroom was based upon group work, there was little opportunity for cooperative learning, and they had relatively few opportunities to make choices related to what they were to learn (as discussed in chapter 4). Students could clearly get the message, then, that their importance was based primarily on group membership, not on their individual qualities.

That message is antithetical to what is usually included in a school's formal statement of mission or philosophy, which typically emphasizes, in part, each individual's unique potential, interests, and capabilities. In this respect there probably was quite a gap between what these schools said they were about and what they were doing in the classrooms.

A second potential message relates to what students might learn from the type of individual the teacher was and what he or she modeled in the classroom. To the students in our sample, the teacher was an all-powerful, all-knowing, very significant individual. The teacher dominated the classroom; determined what was to be learned; paced the activities; was assisted by few, if any, other adults; and otherwise made the important decisions related to classroom life. For this sample of classrooms, the teacher, while powerful, was a supportive, relatively nonthreatening person with whom students seemed to be comfortable.

It would be interesting to know more about what these teachers were like as people, to know their values, views about children, personal interests, and enthusiasm for the teaching profession, for example. (Some of these issues will be examined in chapter 6.) To know how students perceived their teachers in these ways as a person would have significantly extended our understanding of what students might have been learning from the implicit curriculum.

This suggests the importance of the type of individual who teaches in your school. Not only is the quantity of time students spend with teachers important, but the quality of that time must also be of high caliber. Students will tend to learn through the implicit curriculum the traits modeled by your teachers. To be sure that your students are learning from the desired models, your teachers must be selected with great care (see chapter 6). An important task for your school faculty to undertake is to assure in every possible way that your students, who are in the most formative years of their lives, have contact with adults who exhibit the best human traits. Patience, honesty, caring, fallibility, respect, and truthfulness are some of the prime personal attributes that I believe your teachers must exhibit. These are equally important, if not more so, than their academic preparation because of their potential power in the implicit curriculum.

Personal qualities that can significantly affect the quality of classroom life are typically not addressed at all in teacher credentialing. It is left up to the district, and most often to the principal of the individual school, to see that teachers possess the desired types of personal qualities, if they are considered at all. To select the best teachers possible to work with your students in their classrooms is to help assure that the messages students learn from the implicit curriculum about themselves, learning, the school, and about what adults are like will be positive and desirable ones. The power of the teacher is too significant an educational factor in the classroom for you to ignore the personal qualities she or he exhibits.

A third possible message from the context of the classrooms within this sample is that, although schooling occurred in a rather impersonal setting, the people within the classroom were friendly, warm, and somewhat supportive of each other. School was not a terrible place to be for most of these students. While they learned that their teachers were not overly friendly, they also found that they were not hostile or punitive. Although student cliques, competition, and dissonance did exist, students in general were perceived as being friendly and liked. In addition, they were developing at least mildly positive self-concepts. The schools then, were not austere, hostile places that did psychological damage to students. They certainly could have been improved, but most students within them were receiving some important positive messages about themselves and the other people with whom they interacted there.

This view of potential messages, of course, is based on the average of all student responses. There were some individual students, however, who did not perceive their schooling experiences so positively. The challenge for all your teachers is to extend their concern beyond the collective average for the classroom, to the individual student who may not see the school as such a positive place. It is those students who need further attention with regard to the messages they may be receiving from the implicit curriculum. It is those students who may well become the future dropouts. You must strive to make the classroom a comfortable, positive place to be in for all your students.

Challenging Tradition

The potential or real messages of the implicit curriculum must be carefully examined for their impact upon your students and teachers. If the messages are the ones you desire to impart, ways must be found to continue to foster them and even to increase their potential impact. If they are not desirable, existing conditions must be changed so that negative implicit messages will not be transmitted through the physical and social contexts of the classroom. To change the messages of the implicit curriculum may require that you get your teachers to challenge some of their basic assumptions about schooling and get some existing conditions changed.

Tradition structures the implicit and explicit curriculum in very powerful ways. The classrooms in this sample of elementary schools were very traditional in their assumptions about how learning occurs. We have discussed how the physical and social contexts were likely to have affected what students learned. Your physical arrangements and groupings of teachers and students, however, could be very different and thus might better facilitate learning of all types. One very important factor, the computer in the curriculum, may already be well on its way to making alternatives to tradition a necessity. Exploration of how the computer might change schooling could be very productive in helping your faculty challenge traditions.

With the explosion of knowledge that we have witnessed over the past years, the assumption that a single teacher can provide the basic knowledge and support that 25 to 30 students need or want deserves serious examination. Technological advances such as computers, interactive television, and calculators are educational tools that make knowledge more readily available than ever before—knowledge that traditionally was only transmitted by the teacher. Even though these resources have not yet found their way into some elementary classrooms, they will become more and more prevalent in the future.

For now, however, the teacher continues to be the primary source of learning, augmented largely by a textbook in most subject areas, with some supplementary materials used occasionally. As a result, many areas of potential knowledge are never introduced to students. Eisner (1985) refers to this gap as the "null curriculum"—knowledge that never gets offered to students. In the traditional classroom, only that knowledge that your teachers know or that is contained in a textbook becomes the explicit curriculum. This is an extremely limiting assumption and in my judgment is no longer warranted in our age of information. Resources now exist that will enable students to have much more choice regarding what they learn in the explicit curriculum, and these are not only technological advances but many supplementary traditional resources not typically used by the teachers in our sample. Perhaps through the use of those resources, students will also learn from the implicit curriculum that what they are interested in and want to learn does matter and will be honored at school; that they do matter as individuals. Under such conditions, individualization and personalization would become a reality, not merely rhetoric confined only to the intended curriculum. It remains to be seen what kind of an impact this approach to learning might have on all students, especially those at risk.

Planning for technology in your classrooms could be an exciting way to begin real reforms in your curriculum and to provide for a very different kind of interaction among the teachers and students. With the wise use of technological tools, your teachers will be freed to engage in the more human types of interaction which technology cannot do. Students could potentially have more time individually and in small groups with the teacher, in ways that are less judgmental and controlling. That new role for your teachers could dramatically restructure the implicit curriculum for some of your students. Schools must respond to the challenge of technology. Perhaps your teachers will accept the challenge even more seriously and begin to view technology as an opportunity for new and better ways of helping their students learn from the implicit and explicit curriculum.

In addition to the challenges being made from the technological advances in our society, challenges can be made regarding the grouping patterns across and within classrooms. It is possible that more varied human resources could be made available to your students by altering the groupings of adults and students. There are several variations on how teachers and students can be grouped, other than in self-contained classrooms. Team teaching, for example, which never has been fully explored by the schools, would be a viable alternative to the traditional grouping patterns seen in these schools. Others, such as departmentalization, may decrease the flexibility of the classroom more than is desired, especially for the early years, but modified organizational patterns departing from the self-contained classroom can minimize this limitation.

More challenging ways of grouping students and teachers at your school could be identified, discussed, and experimented with as ways of better facilitating the desired learning from both the implicit and explicit curriculum. Making other teachers available to assist students with their learning brings to the classroom additional areas of expertise with which to augment the explicit curriculum. Contact with other teachers also would provide students with different role models, opportunities to relate successfully to different adults, and various models of the same basic human qualities that you want your students to develop. Important knowledge about human interactions and adults could thus be gained by your students, through deliberate planning of the implicit curriculum.

Even within self-contained classrooms, the traditional modes of grouping could be challenged. Other grouping patterns than just a large or total group must be present if important learning in the explicit and implicit curriculum is to be fostered. The current interest, for example, in cooperative learning was not evident in this sample of classrooms.

Students were learning mainly in large groups what was being presented by the teacher. They received little individual help as they pursued
their studies. Little wonder that some students perceived the classroom
as competitive. They were learning about competition from the implicit
curriculum and did not appear to have an opportunity to learn about
cooperation within the classroom. If your school has overlooked this
factor, it could be having a significant impact on both the explicit and
implicit curriculum. If other grouping patterns were used, your students could receive more help and individualization in their work in the
explicit curriculum and also learn from the implicit curriculum that
they are important and do matter as individuals.

Unless you examine the traditional self-contained classroom setup
for its strengths and limitations and propose modifications and alternatives to it, any other changes you make may continue to result in the
restricted learning and limited curricula now offered in too many
schools. Even as you challenge some of the fundamental assumptions
upon which elementary education is based, you must monitor any
changes you make, to insure that you have not created any new unwant-
ed messages. Above all else, the classrooms in your school must become
healthy, exciting, challenging, stimulating places to live and learn, for
your teachers and students. Any assumption or practice that limits this
should be identified, challenged, and changed.

Another assumption of schooling that you may want to challenge is
that the only thing that matters is how the teacher facilitates learning,
especially if that view is restricted to the currently popular definition of
academic learning time (Denham & Lieberman, 1980). Although ALT
is basic to some important goals of schooling, always of primary and
equal importance are human relations within the classroom. Out of
these interactions comes learning perhaps even more essential than
knowledge in the subject areas. From these interactions your students
will learn whether they are adequate human beings able to cope with
the demands of schooling; they will form lasting views of themselves as
learners and as people. They will learn to view other students and
teachers as being friendly and supportive or competitive, cliquish, and
unreasonably demanding. Social interactions in your classrooms must
never be minimized, even for the sake of ALT and increased achievement test scores; they must always be of the highest quality. Assumptions and practices that diminish the quality of the social interactions of
your classrooms must be questioned and corrected. Your teachers must
interact with students with warmth, openness, acceptance, trust, respect, and nurturance. Then your students will learn to see themselves
and others as important, equal, friendly, and worthy human beings
possessing unique strengths and limitations.

Schools are not, and must not be considered as, factories where only the intellectual output of students is valued or where the best worker is the teacher, who provides only one type of learning, albeit highly desirable, for students. Schools are places where students spend a large part of their formative years. The time spent by them in your school must be productive for a wide range of learning and must be of a highly positive social and emotional, as well as intellectual, quality. None of these aspects of the school and classroom contexts must be neglected at the expense of the others. All must be carefully nurtured in your classrooms. The quality of life as defined through the physical and social contexts of the classroom must receive your most careful attention as you develop your plan for curriculum improvement.

CHAPTER 6

Teachers in the Elementary School

We have seen in the preceding chapters the power that teachers have in the elementary classroom. They are the prime decision makers for their classrooms — affecting what students learn in the explicit and implicit curriculum and the quality of their lives at school. We have discussed how teachers control and direct all major aspects of the classroom, through their values, interests, and abilities. The teacher *is* the school for most students, since they have little or no opportunity during the school day to interact with any other adult, especially not another who has the power of the teacher.

Given this significance and power, it is clear that your teachers are an important factor in school improvement. To know who your teachers are — their personal qualities, their professional preparation and skills, how they continue to grow as educators, and their educational beliefs and values — is to understand more fully their potential impact upon the curriculum and your students. They are, indeed, powerful determinants of the quality of education your students will receive. But their characteristics and beliefs are important not only to the classroom but to the culture of the school as well. Thus, selecting the teachers for your school is one of the most fundamental decisions to be made about schooling and one to which you should give careful deliberation.

This chapter focuses upon the teachers in our sample and their impact on the curriculum. As we discuss the data on our sample of teachers in an effort to learn more about them, you might raise similar questions about your teachers.

- How committed to the teaching profession are they?
- How well prepared are they for their positions?
- What opportunities do they have for continued growth as professional educators?
- What are their educational beliefs?
- How do they perceive themselves as members of a faculty and in relation to school administrators?
- What kinds of problems do they perceive at their schools?

- What kind of impact might teachers' characteristics have on the curriculum?

The answers you receive to these types of questions should be closely scrutinized to be sure that your teachers have the characteristics and attributes you value so that your students will receive a quality education in every respect. The significance of the teacher in the educative processes must be considered in any improvement effort. Careful attention to who your teachers are and what type you would like to have in your school should also enable you to select new teachers more carefully and help the teachers at your school continue to grow as educators.

We examined a variety of data about our teachers and will begin here by discussing some basic demographic data. Then we will examine their professional preparation, the opportunities they had for continued professional growth, their satisfaction with their careers in teaching, their perceptions of the influence they had over selected important aspects of schooling, their perceptions of potential problems faced by many schools today, and their educational beliefs regarding classroom practices. The chapter concludes with a discussion about what is needed to help your teachers continue their growth as professional educators.

PERSONAL CHARACTERISTICS AND PROFESSIONAL PREPARATION

Demographic Data

Demographic data can be helpful in describing the members of a group. In our elementary school sample there were 286 teachers who taught grades 1 through 6 (Goodlad, Sirotnik, & Overman, 1979). Listings of percentage breakdowns within categories are given in Figure 6.1. As can be seen, there are some distinct trends in these teachers' demographic characteristics. Nearly two-thirds of the teachers were under 40 years old, and over two-thirds were married. Almost 90% of the teachers were women, and four out of five were white.

The teachers clearly were not overpaid; on the contrary, they were for the most part appallingly underpaid. Half reported household incomes of under $20,000, and two-thirds under $25,000. It is apparent that the salaries cannot be a major source of satisfaction for these teachers; other factors must have been operating to keep them in the teaching profession.

Over half of the teachers classified themselves as politically moder-

Figure 6.1 Demographic Characteristics of Teachers in the Sample

Age (%)		Sex (%)		Marital Status (%)	
21-29	32.7%	Male	13.0%	Single	23.6
30-39	30.9	Female	87.0	Married	70.7
40-49	18.0			Other	5.8
50-59	14.4				
60 +	4.0				

Race/Ethnicity (%)		Family Income (%)	
White	80.0	$5,000-9,999	10.1
Black	12.0	$10,000-14,999	24.2
Asian	1.4	$15,000-19,999	16.6
Mexican-American	3.9	$20,000-24,999	17.0
Other	1.8	$25,000 or more	32.1

Source: Tye, 1980

ate, and the rest were divided nearly equally between the conservative and liberal camps. Very few said they were strongly at either end of the political spectrum.

While most of these characteristics suggest that teachers were not out of the ordinary demographically, others must be closely examined for their impact on the type of schooling the students probably received. For example, the small number of male elementary teachers could be viewed as a serious limitation. Students lacked the opportunity to inter-act with males and missed having them as role models in their very formative years. In addition, students may well have concluded that teaching in the elementary school is a career suited only for females. This would be a highly undesirable message from the implicit curriculum, if indeed students did learn this.

Another limitation of this sample was the paucity of minority-group teachers. With primarily white teachers in evidence at school, other very erroneous messages could be given regarding who is qualified to be a teacher. Further, while minority students, in particular, are denied role models, all students are denied the opportunity to interact with a variety of different people. That void could be an important aspect of their education.

Finally, with the low incomes reported, I wonder how many of these teachers were able to devote their exclusive attention to teaching as a profession. It is probable that some, if not many, of these teachers had to have other sources of income in order to maintain a reasonable standard of living.

These categories represent the kinds of demographic data you may want to collect in order to describe the teachers in your school. Their characteristics could well have an important influence upon the education of your students. Since teachers do have such a powerful impact on schooling, new ones need to be chosen very carefully to balance in desirable ways the teachers who are already at your school.

Professional Preparation

Our teachers were well prepared for their profession, as can be seen in the following list of highest degree attained; over 99% had at least a bachelor's degree, and nearly one-quarter had master's degrees:

High school diploma	0.4%
Associate degree	0.4%
Bachelor's degree	76.6%
Master's degree	22.0%
Doctorate	0.7%

The teachers' college majors and minors give some insight into their areas of general preparation. As shown in Table 6.1, slightly less than half of the teachers majored or minored in English, and a comparable percentage majored or minored in general education. About one-third majored or minored in social sciences. The arts, physical science, math, physical education, and special education were less well represented (J. Wright, 1980b).

Of those who had pursued professional preparation beyond their initial credential, 48.6% had done work in teaching methods and about 35.7% had studied particular subject areas. Another 6.7% had studied administration, and 9% had pursued other postcredential work (Tye,

Table 6.1 Teachers' Professional Studies and Feelings of Adequacy

	College Major or Minor (%)	Postcredential Work (%)	Feel Inadequately Prepared (%)
English	46.5	44.8	4.7
General Education	43.2	33.3	n.a.
Social Sciences	34.9	23.2	4.6
Arts	21.8	21.3	29.1
Physical Sciences	17.9	18.8	23.3
Math	11.6	23.8	2.0
Special Education	7.5	16.3	4.5
Physical Education	7.4	8.5	18.6

Sources: J. Wright, 1980b; Tye, 1980

1980). This group of teachers, then, had continued their postcredential work in areas that would directly assist them in their classroom work. Few seemed to be seeking administrative positions or other jobs that would take them out of the classroom.

Most teachers who had done postcredential work in a specific subject area had studied English or general education (see Table 6.1). The trends in postcredential work by subject area followed the pattern of college majors, with one exception: There were twice as many teachers who did postgraduate work in math than there were math majors. Nevertheless, English and general education accounted for the academic work of the majority of teachers, both during college and their postcredential work.

Thus, although most of these teachers had the expected amount of education, a bachelor's degree, the balance of work in subject-area preparation was skewed. These schools had little expert help from teachers who had majored in subject areas such as math, the arts, science, and physical education. This could have been a factor that accounted for the imbalanced curriculum in these subject areas. Teachers may have been reluctant to teach areas in which they had little preparation. Unless the districts assisted them in becoming better prepared, as many often do, particularly in math, our teachers were not likely to offer strong curricula in these areas.

The professional preparation of your teachers is worthy of your special attention. It can significantly influence the balance of the curriculum offered to your students. Any attempt to develop curriculum at your school will require teachers with some expertise in the subject areas. The teacher with strong preparation in English, math, social studies, art, or physical education is in a position to offer leadership in curriculum improvement efforts within that subject. Where there is no expertise at your school in a particular subject, the chances are that curriculum improvement efforts in it will not be strong. Selecting teachers with varying expertise in their professional preparation could be an important consideration when filling new or vacant faculty positions.

When asked specifically how prepared they were to teach the various subject areas for which they were responsible, the great majority of our teachers responded that they considered themselves qualified. As shown in Table 6.1, over 95% of those who were doing so felt adequately prepared to teach English, social sciences, math, and special education. Less than one-quarter felt ill prepared to teach physical sciences or physical education. Only among those teaching the arts did the proportion who felt inadequately prepared approach one-third. These data strongly suggest that most of our teachers perceived themselves to be qualified to teach what their assignments included, even though their academic majors in college may not have prepared them. Perhaps they were receiving special preparation in subject areas from other educational sources. We will examine this possibility in a later section.

The teachers in our sample were asked to choose the one factor that was most important in leading them to enter the field of education. Their responses were distributed as follows:

Subject/teaching interest	24.6%
Inherent professional values	16.8%
Help others	17.9%
Influenced by others	14.3%
Like children	14.6%
Working conditions	6.1%
Other	2.9%
Economic	2.1%
Scholarship	0.7%

Our teachers, then reported they entered their profession primarily for noble reasons: interest in a subject area, to help others, inherent professional values, and because they liked children. Economics and job conditions attracted few (Tye, 1980).

Overall, this sample of teachers felt adequately educated for their careers as teachers, at least initially. Nearly all had at least a bachelor's degree, often in English or general studies, and they further perceived themselves to be prepared to teach the areas they found themselves teaching. They were attracted to teaching for positive reasons: their interest in a subject area, a desire to work with children, and to help others. These conditions would seem to be a solid start for our teachers and represent important and desirable characteristics of any group of teachers. But the initial work of teacher preparation must be followed by continued professional development after teachers are on the job. What of their continuing development as teachers? What opportunities did they have to extend their initial preparation as teachers?

Opportunities for Continued Professional Growth

Teachers usually have a variety of opportunities for continuing their professional growth after they are on the job. We asked our teachers about some of the most common ones: their involvement in staff development or inservice programs and workshops, their membership in professional organizations, and to what extent they read professional publications.

Inservice Programs and Workshops. We asked our teachers what types of professional programs they had attended during the past 3 years and the general focus of the programs. Staff development programs at the local school and district or county level were the most popular sources of inservice education, much more than programs through outside agencies (Tye, 1980). Five general topics — teaching methods or strategies, classroom management, adult group dynamics (human relationships), behavioral objectives and evaluation, and curriculum development — accounted for most of the content, though in no case did more than 25% of the teachers report that they had attended a workshop on one of these topics. Child growth and development and cross-cultural education were rather infrequently attended (less than 10% of the teachers responded to each of these topics).

In the specific subject fields, not surprisingly, the largest percentage of teachers reported attending English or reading/language arts (47%) staff development programs sponsored by the school, district, county, or an outside agency. Percentages for the other subject areas were: the arts, 36%; physical education, 33%; math, 30%; science, 19%; and social studies, 16%. Most of these staff development programs were sponsored by the district or county, though there were two exceptions: the arts, where more programs were attended through outside agencies than through the district or county, and physical education, in which most programs were sponsored by the school or an outside agency (Tye, 1980).

Nearly 40% of the teachers also reported attendance at college-level workshops in English, followed by 25% each in mathematics and the arts. Relatively few teachers reported attending workshops in physical education (14%), social science (12%), or physical science (8%) (J. Wright, 1980b). These inservice programs and workshops may well account for why the teachers perceived themselves as being prepared to teach the subjects they found themselves teaching, regardless of their academic preparation in college.

Teachers, then, attended programs and workshops directly related to their ongoing daily work: managing the classroom and teaching the subjects for which they were responsible, particularly those associated with "the basics" in the curriculum. Attendance at inservice programs and workshops for curricular areas not considered among "the basics" was not strong. Programs in child growth and development were also not attended by many teachers, nor was multicultural education. We do not know why they were not more popular, but it is puzzling to me that these two fundamental topics in human development and schooling in a democracy were slighted. Perhaps the teachers did not perceive them as relevant to the ongoing work of their classrooms since they were not subject areas that they had to teach.

Overall, however, only modest percentages of our teachers from any single school attended staff development programs. For most schools, 30% or fewer teachers responded that they had attended an inservice program. That is a low percentage of teachers who took advantage of — and responsibility for — continuing their professional growth. It would be interesting to know why more did not attend. Unfortunately, we did not ask about the quality of the programs or the degree of encouragement that the teachers might have received to attend inservice programs. These could have been important factors in the low attendance.

Should you find comparable data at your school, they would be worthy of further investigation. Your teachers can benefit greatly from well-designed, pertinent inservice programs and workshops. If they do not avail themselves of the opportunities for continued growth that these represent, you should find out why. Perhaps they need to receive greater encouragement and incentives for attendance, or perhaps the programs need to be redirected to be more useful to your teachers. Without some involvement in ways to continue their professional growth, your teachers are not likely to increase the skills and abilities they need to design and implement the kind of curriculum you would like your school to have.

Professional Organizations and Publications. Another avenue for continued education is through membership in the many existing professional organizations. Most elementary teachers in our sample reported that they had joined professional organizations, and 42% reported membership in three or four (Tye, 1980). Less than one-fifth (18%) said they had joined no professional organizations. Slightly less than half (44%) of the teachers further reported that their organizational membership had some effect on their professional growth, while 22% said it had very little or no effect. Similar percentages of teachers reported that their working conditions had been influenced by their professional organizations. Most teachers (42%) said professional memberships had some effect, while 21% said they had a lot, 20% claimed very little, and 18% claimed no effect upon their working conditions.

Not only did some of our teachers attend inservice programs and join professional organizations, they also read educational books, articles, and reports. The majority, 64%, had read nine or more such publications during the previous year. Less than one-fifth (17%) said they read only five to eight such publications, and another 16% had read only one to four during the previous year. Only 2% reported they had read none.

Implications. Beyond their immediate work in the classroom, then, the majority of our teachers made attempts to continue to grow and develop in some way as professional educators. Some attended staff development programs, more joined professional organizations that were judged to be of some benefit, and many read educational books, articles, or reports.

The extent to which these efforts directly affected their classroom skills and expertise, however, did not seem to be very great, for reasons we discussed in chapters 2 and 3. In spite of their beliefs that they were prepared, we found evidence that they were not as prepared as they should have been. There were serious gaps between the goals they said they wanted and what they were doing in their classrooms. This may have been because the quality of the programs for continuing their professional education was not as high as it should have been.

It is possible that at least one other condition was operating to keep the teachers from being as prepared as I think they ought to have been: Their avenues of professional growth were not based in their classrooms. To receive help in their continued growth, teachers usually had to leave where they worked and receive their help elsewhere. As noted in chapter 5, about half of the teachers taught alone in a self-contained classroom (Tye, 1980). Very few of them (2%) reported that they received regular help from a specialist or even had some assistance and stimulation from a student teacher (1%). Less than one-fifth of them (18%) said they were a member of a teaching team, taught in a self-contained classroom with even informal help from one or more teachers (15%), or taught with one or more aides (14%). Few teachers in this sample, then, were receiving any stimulation or help in their classroom. They were very isolated from other people and alternative classroom practices, both of which could help them grow. This isolation must be carefully examined for its impact on the curriculum.

If a strong, balanced curriculum is desired at your school, your teachers must have some degree of preparation in all of the subject areas they are expected to teach. They must have help in other areas, such as the implicit curriculum, that do not receive much attention in the short preservice program in teacher education. Preservice education is a place to begin the development of a teacher, but opportunities for growth in all the areas of classroom living and learning must be continued after graduation. A carefully planned, effective staff development program is needed which, at least in part, occurs directly in teachers' classrooms and is given by professionals who have ideas and can help them right where the action is. Such inservice help, centering on both the explicit and implicit curriculum, would be fundamental to helping your teachers continue to grow in their work, if they are as isolated in a self-contained classroom as our teachers were.

Many scholars have deplored the lack of peer communication among most teachers, and their studies have carefully identified how the self-contained classroom limits professional growth and development (e.g., Lieberman & Miller, 1984; Lortie, 1975). Alternatives to this structure were briefly proposed in the previous chapter, including team teaching or departmentalization. These involve teachers teaching in their areas of specialization and students sometimes moving from classroom to classroom, or at least changing teachers, in order to experience a more enriched and better balanced curriculum. In addition, the students have opportunities to relate to more than just a single adult during the day, thus enhancing their understanding of human relationships and expanding the kinds of role models from whom they can learn.

But these advantages for such changes must be weighed against the disadvantages, and any fundamental change in a process as complex as schooling usually has both strengths and weaknesses. You must decide whether the change is a worthy one for your school. Both of the alternatives for organizing teachers and learning—team teaching and departmentalization—fragment the students' day into time blocks, which further increases the regimentation of learning into discrete areas of content and artificial time barriers. The opportunities for students to integrate their learning in various subject areas are considerably reduced. Further, teachers do not get to know individual students as well. They might lack important knowledge of students which would enable them to relate more effectively to them, for either learning or personal purposes, unless there is close teacher communication within the teams or departments.

Another disadvantage to these organizational arrangements is that they still may not allow your teachers to have sufficient opportunities to learn from each other, although they may have more opportunities than they would in an isolated, self-contained classroom. Even though reor-

ganizing the school may be of some help to teachers for increased stimulation from their peers, additional opportunities will also be needed to
help your teachers in their continued professional development.

How teachers are prepared as professional educators and organized
to teach in your school are very significant decisions which affect the
quality of the education and the daily lives of your students at school.
These decisions must be made carefully after a full review of the advantages and disadvantages to the teachers and students who work in the
school. The decisions you make are critical, but they are not as clear-cut
as some authors in education would have us believe. To make an informed decision, you must first decide what kind of an education and
what quality of life you want your students to have. Then the organization of the school and the continued professional preparation of your
teachers must follow your vision, in order to maximize it. To decide
upon the organization and professional growth of teachers without a
knowledge of what you want in curriculum is to have only part of the
plan for improvement.

Career Satisfaction

Related to our investigation of why the teachers entered the teaching profession and how they continued their growth as professional
educators is the question of whether their career expectations had been
fulfilled. Were they pleased with their decision to become teachers, or
did they have regrets about it? Over three-fourths of our teachers
(79.9%) said their expectations had been fulfilled, and a comparable
number (76.5%) said they would choose education again as their profession. This finding is quite contrary to some of the literature today citing
teacher burn-out and dissatisfaction with teaching as a career. Overall,
our teachers were relatively well satisfied with their choice to become a
teacher.

Since teaching as a career is not without its frustrations, we asked
what might cause our teachers to leave the profession. When asked what
their most likely reason would be for leaving their present position, 38%
cited personal frustration or dissatisfaction with their own job performance (Tye, 1980). To earn more money was the next most often cited
reason, but only 18%, or less than half of the percentage in the first
category, said they would leave for this. Another 14% said they would
seek a job with higher status than teaching currently possesses. A difficult student population and personal conflict with the administration
would cause only relatively small percentages of the teachers to leave
(11% in each case). Even smaller percentages would leave because of

severe staff conflict (6%) or inadequate plant facilities or materials to use (3%).

Lack of professional success, then, would be the primary cause for our teachers to leave education, with more money and greater status trailing behind as reasons for leaving. In-school reasons, even difficult student populations and interpersonal conflicts, were cited as reasons for leaving by rather small numbers. It is interesting to note that large numbers of teachers did not respond to some of the in-school causes that might normally be thought of as reasons for leaving the profession. The majority of our teachers experienced personal satisfaction with their decision to go into teaching.

Synthesis of Characteristics

On the whole, our teachers appeared to be relatively young, adequately prepared (in their perceptions), rather poorly paid, largely white females, moderate in politics, motivated by noble reasons to become teachers, and a fairly well-satisfied group of professionals who continued developing their skills and abilities through some channels. With some exceptions, the teachers reflected some very positive demographic and professional factors that portray the type of people I would like to see working with our young people. There were some limitations as we noted earlier, such as the numbers of minorities and men included, but, overall, this sample of schools had a personally and educationally attractive group of teachers on many counts. To expect a quality education for students based upon such positive teacher characteristics would not appear to be unreasonable.

The important questions for you to answer now are

- What are your teachers like?
- Do they reflect the personal and professional qualities of the type of teachers you want in your school?
- Most importantly, will those qualities provide the foundation for the type of curriculum you want your students to have?

TEACHERS' IMPACT ON THE PROFESSIONAL MILIEU

The personal characteristics and professional preparation of your teachers provide only the foundation for the success and satisfaction of your teachers and students. Other variables will also significantly affect how your teachers operate in their classrooms and in the school: perceptions of their influence, the kinds of problems they believe your school has, and their educational beliefs about what ought to occur in the schooling process. These are the topics to which we now turn.

Teacher Perceptions of Their Influence in Selected Areas

As reported in chapter 2, our teachers perceived themselves as having a lot of control over some basic decisions in their planning and teaching. In addition to these, we asked them about their influence over other aspects of schooling: curriculum, instruction, and pupil behavior; communication with parents; dress codes; teaching assignments; staff meetings and extracurricular activities; community related issues and activities; fiscal management of school resources; selection and evaluation of teaching assistants; and selection and evaluation of professional staff members. Out of 33 items (clustered into the nine subscales named above), the items composing the subscale dealing with curriculum, instruction, and pupil behavior were the only ones over which the teachers perceived themselves as having a lot of influence (D. Wright, 1980b). In three of the subscales — fiscal management, selection and evaluation of teaching assistants, and selection and evaluation of professional staff members — the teachers believed they had no influence. In the remaining five subscales, the teachers perceived themselves as having at least some influence. The strongest scale in these five was communication with parents, in which teachers felt they had some influence and approached having a lot of influence. The other four subscales also reflected some perceived influence, but leaned toward no influence rather than a lot of influence.

Not surprisingly, our teachers perceived themselves as a faculty having more influence over decisions closest to their classrooms: curriculum, instruction, student behavior, and communication with parents. They had some influence over dress codes, teaching assignments, meetings and extracurricular activities, and community related activities. The teachers did not perceive themselves, however, as having any influence over fiscal concerns of the school or selection and evaluation of staff members, either teaching assistants or full-time teachers. The aspects over which they thought they had no control are significant areas in which teachers have vested interests, however. This pattern of influence suggests very strongly the existence of a management-and-labor approach to the operation of a school, rather than the collegial arrangement that is found in higher education, particularly with the selection of personnel. I believe the lack of involvement for teachers in these significant areas must be challenged as to its appropriateness for any group of professional educators.

The divisiveness of the labor-and-management model has, in my opinion, been heightened by the inroads made by labor unions into education. The school is modeled after a factory in which laborers have a specific task to perform but little input into policy and fiscal decisions except through union activities. Whether this ought to be the model has been strongly challenged by Eisner (1985) and debated by Lortie (1975). Perhaps a more collegial approach to the administration of a school would produce a different climate in schools — a climate where different types of professional educators with different expertise work in concert to help students receive the best possible education. An atmosphere where teachers are very involved in helping select their peers, for example, might foster a greater commitment to the quality of the school and their teaching responsibilities. It could also help further their professional growth regarding what is important in schooling and how teacher characteristics can contribute to a student's education. This approach has been tried in some schools, with excellent results (Sanders & Schwab, 1981). Similarly, some degree of influence over how the limited resources of a school will get spent may well sensitize teachers to the importance of making wise decisions about the resources on a schoolwide basis and make them less self-centered in what they expect for their own classrooms.

The spending of the always limited resources of the school and the selection of colleagues are two areas in which teachers have vested interests and should have some degree of control, or at least some influence, in my opinion. The degree of influence teachers feel they have over important school matters can be a pervasive factor in increasing their commitment to improving the curriculum and the quality of life at school.

Let us consider just one example of the pervasiveness of this issue. The perceived pattern of lack of teacher influence beyond the classroom in our sample resembled the way students reported their influence over classroom decisions. As our teachers were treated, so they treated their students. You will want the practices by your administrators and teachers to exemplify the values and attitudes they espouse. If your teachers are valued professionals, opportunities for participation in decisions that affect them must be provided. If your students are expected to develop decision-making skills, learn how to learn, and foster their own interests and potentials, they must be allowed to make significant decisions about their curricula. Schooling is too often an other-directed and controlled process for both of the major groups, teachers and students. This has an impact on the quality of the education received in school and on the daily lives of teachers and students. The impact is neither desirable nor educationally defensible, in my opinion. Ways of providing greater influence and control for both teachers and students in more areas must be found if our schools are to fulfill the functions expected of them.

These issues, however, are debatable, and you will need to answer them for your school. What aspects of schooling do you and your teachers believe teachers should be involved in and to what extent, and what aspects are not so important for them to be involved in? Teacher input in the areas of curriculum, instruction, and communications with parents, of course, must occur. What about areas of fiscal responsibility, staff meetings, selection of personnel, and community related activities? Are these ones from which teachers should be excluded? For me, to have a teaching staff excluded from them is to diminish the definition of teachers as professionals. The implications of not having your teachers involved in such important areas should be examined very closely by you and your faculty, as you attempt to define your teachers' roles as professional educators.

Teacher Perceptions of School-Related Problems

Your teachers are a major component of the larger context of schooling, as well as of their classroom context. As such, the school is directly affected by any schoolwide problems that teachers believe you have, even though the problems may not be directly rooted in the classroom context or under the direct influence of individual teachers. Thus, their views could be important to your curriculum improvement plan.

Our teachers were asked to rate a series of potential problems of the school as being major, minor, or not a problem. (The problems listed were in addition to the problems of poor curriculum and poor teachers or teaching, as reported in chapter 2.) All of the potential problems named were rated by teachers as either minor or as not a problem (Overman, 1980b). Heading the list of minor problems were student misbehavior, size of the school and the classes, and lack of parent interest in the school. Following these were lack of student interest, inadequate resources, student language problems, how the school was organized, policies and regulations that interfere with education, lack of teacher discipline for students, staff relations, administration of the school, and lack of staff interest in good school/community relations. Those areas not perceived as problems included prejudice or racial conflict, drug and alcohol use, busing for integration, desegregation, and standards for graduation and academic requirements. It is interesting to note that our sample of schools was not experiencing some of the major problems being faced by other schools, such as racial conflict, drug and alcohol use, and desegregation issues.

Some of the problems our teachers perceived as the biggest problems, but still as minor ones, were those least under their control — poor student behavior (assuming this means the way in which students generally act inside and outside of school), size of the school and the classes, and lack of parental interest. Lack of student interest (assuming that motivation is an important task for the teacher), poor curriculum, and poor teaching are those over which a teacher has considerable control. These problem areas, however, tended to be on the lower or less intense end of the scale of minor problems. The social problems associated with integration and drug and alcohol abuse were not perceived as problems at all by this sample of elementary teachers. Our teachers seemed to perceive the problems their schools faced in a similar way as the parents did (see chapter 4). Parents and teachers seemed to agree that, although the schools had areas in need of improvement, many problems that might be expected to be serious in some schools were not perceived as major ones for these schools.

Our schools did not seem to possess, then, any overwhelming problems that might have diverted their attention away from improving classroom practice. Even though some of the minor problems were not directly located in their classrooms, had they addressed and successfully resolved them (if only to reduce their intensity), their schools would have been even better places for students and teachers. These schools clearly were not perceived as unpleasant or difficult places for teachers or students to live and work (also see chapter 5).

It would be interesting to explore with your faculty and parents what problems they think your school might have. You may want to add other problems to our list of potential problems. It will not be enough, however, just to have the problems identified. Next steps for your faculty would be to address ways in which the problems might be reduced in intensity or perhaps eliminated completely. Discussions in which you address the problems could be very powerful ones in helping your teachers consider and develop an increasing commitment to the organic wholeness of a school beyond the immediate concerns of their classroom.

It is not enough that teachers focus only on their own classrooms, although that clearly will be their major concern. They must also remember that they exist in a larger whole called the school. Schools, as they reflect the broader society, will always have problems, but your faculty may find that they have more power and influence over reducing the intensity of problems than they thought. To address the problems your faculty identifies, you may need to involve the resources of the larger community, such as museums, police services, community organizations, and counseling services for families. Do not overlook any such possible resources in resolving the problems your school may have. Your school, in addition to your teachers and students, needs nurturing and improvement. The improvement of your school as a place for teachers and students to interact and learn will undoubtedly be reflected in making their classrooms better places, too.

Educational Beliefs of Teachers

The vision of what your faculty would like to have occur at their school and in their classrooms has been emphasized in a number of places throughout this book. It will depend, in part, upon the educational beliefs of your teachers. The importance of their beliefs about what schooling ought to be will play a key role in developing your curriculum improvement plan.

Our teachers were asked to respond to a set of 21 statements regarding their educational beliefs. Their responses consisted of six options: "strongly agree," "moderately agree," "mildly agree," "mildly disagree," "moderately disagree," and "strongly disagree." The responses indicated that the teachers held varied beliefs about the process of schooling; that is, there was little consensus among teachers' responses (D. Wright, 1980a). When agreement did occur, however, it was rather strong. Interestingly, the responses of our elementary teachers about their educational beliefs did not vary significantly from the responses of the sample of secondary teachers.

The 21 items formed two major scales reflecting either a progressive or a traditional orientation to education. These two scales were further subdivided into two subscales each, regarding basic skills and teacher control reflecting traditional beliefs, and regarding student concern and student participation reflecting progressive beliefs.

Overall, the teachers either mildly or moderately agreed with statements reflecting *both* the traditional and the progressive orientation at the same time. Our teachers agreed more strongly, however, with the progressive beliefs than the traditional beliefs. More specifically, the teachers agreed either mildly or moderately with the traditional beliefs of teacher control and the teaching of basic skills, and at the same time agreed either mildly or moderately (though overall somewhat more strongly) with the progressive beliefs of student participation and concern for student welfare.

At first, the dual nature of the teachers' responses to the teacher belief scales seemed surprising. Were our teachers schizophrenic, unsure of what they believed, lacking an integrated set of beliefs, or drawing upon different belief systems for different purposes in the education of children? The data, of course, did not directly answer these questions, but the answer is likely to be the latter explanation. Teachers' reported beliefs about education, as well as the old adage that elementary teachers teach children, not content, would suggest the need for some classroom practices based on progressive beliefs. A concern for students and student participation in their education would be very much in keeping with the desire to help children grow and mature in many ways, rather than to emphasize content exclusively. Further, we saw in chapter 5 that students perceived that their teachers had concern for them as students. Unfortunately, many practices we documented in the classrooms did not reflect the reported belief in student participation.

On the other hand, there are strong societal expectations that teachers are to be in control of their classrooms and teach the students the basics — the important skills of communication and the intellectual processes, and a body of content that will prepare them to participate as educated citizens. These expectations are usually met through the teaching of traditional subject areas, and teachers are often held accountable for them through standardized tests at the state and local levels. Further, it is believed that these subjects are learned best when the teacher is fully in control of the classroom and instruction. The societal pressure for having the subject areas taught in a form recognizable and accountable to the lay public dare not be overlooked today by teachers.

Most teachers, of course, would not choose to neglect or ignore these responsibilities, even if the societal pressure were lessened. They, too, want students to have the basic knowledge and intellectual abilities required to cope with our society today. Both public pressure and their own personal beliefs, then, may have helped our teachers maintain their traditional orientation to educational practices.

But the fact that most teachers also clearly indicated a desire that the curriculum should do more than just fulfill the intellectual function should never be overlooked (see chapter 2). They also supported the personal and social functions of schooling. Perhaps this is why they also professed progressive beliefs about educating students, which are not served well by the exclusive teaching of the traditional subject areas. Their progressive beliefs should have been reflected in their classrooms through more student participation in learning tasks, opportunities that cannot be provided by only teaching traditional content. Thus, only part of their progressive beliefs found their way into practice in the classrooms, partly because the subject areas were the dominant form of organizing the curriculum. Only a few of the strongest and most creative teachers in any school dare acknowledge that there are alternative ways to design and organize curricula to meet better the other desirable functions of schooling.

The duality of the teachers' responses becomes more understandable when the expectations and pressures of our society and the teachers' beliefs about the traditional functions of the curriculum are coupled with their beliefs that the curriculum also ought to meet the social and personal functions of schooling, as well as with their desires to enter the profession so that they could work with children in ways to help them grow and develop as people. The combination of these influences encouraged both a traditional and a progressive orientation to schooling. In fact, the strength and value of the elementary school in today's world may well depend upon the coexistence of both sets of beliefs and the development of compatible practices, as the schools are needed to serve more and more functions for our society.

Should you find comparable data from your teachers, the challenge will be to help them find classroom practices that are more compatible with their belief systems than our teachers did. You will need to help them improve how they teach the basics to their students and maintain a proper level of control over their classrooms. At the same time, they need ways of showing their concern for the students, both as learners and as people, and of providing appropriate opportunities for their students to make some meaningful decisions about their learning. In this way, you will help your teachers close the gap between what they believe and what they do in their classrooms, providing clear evidence that your school is, indeed, working toward curriculum improvement.

THE TEACHER AS PROFESSIONAL EDUCATOR

Much of the data presented in this chapter, and some in preceding ones, raise the question as to what it means to be a professional educator. What specialized knowledge, skills, and values they must possess; how they continue the education they began in preservice studies; what kinds of decisions they should be able to make; under what conditions they should work; and how much satisfaction they experience from being a teacher all relate to what being a professional teacher means. This section summarizes some of our relevant data and relates them to how you can help your teachers become even better professional educators.

Much of the data from the Study of Schooling clearly showed that our teachers had many characteristics that would help them be effective professional educators. Nearly all of them possessed at least a bachelor's degree, and most received their degrees in subject areas of the elementary school curriculum which they had to teach, or else in general studies, which undoubtedly included many areas of the elementary school curriculum. Further, they believed they were prepared to teach most of the subject areas they found themselves teaching. Their preservice work was augmented by several, but limited, avenues of continued professional growth available after they began teaching: staff development programs, workshops, professional associations, and professional journals and magazines. They held fairly firm beliefs about classroom practices. They reported at least mild satisfaction with their careers as teachers, and many indicated they would leave only if personal satisfaction with their professional performance were reduced.

From our prior data and discussions, however, there were limitations with viewing these teachers as fully functioning professional educators. It is apparent that these teachers did not exhibit all of the abilities needed to implement the balanced curriculum they said they wanted nor to implement classroom practices that were consistent with their educational beliefs. Further, they did not take full advantage of opportunities for continued growth in learning how to make a wide range of professional decisions more effectively. The numbers of teachers who attended staff development programs and workshops were depressingly low.

Their working conditions also kept them from functioning fully as professional educators. Teachers were isolated in their classrooms, had little or no contact with other teachers during the day, had limited contact with administrators presumed to be instructional leaders, did not often use supervisory help from the district, and depended largely upon themselves and their students as determinants of what was taught. Avenues such as these for possible growth for these teachers as professional educators were much too limited. Curriculum improvement is not likely to occur under these conditions.

Another limitation to our teachers' functioning as professional educators was the very low salaries they reported. Clearly, they were not being adequately paid or recognized financially as professionals. Teachers' unions have helped teachers everywhere successfully make this limitation known to state legislators, district administrators, and the general public. Teachers' salaries are slowly improving, but the gap between what they receive and how much they deserve for the fundamental role they play in our society remains depressingly wide. As teachers receive more equitable salaries, the incentive will be greater for them to be even more qualified as professional educators in every respect.

These limitations of our teachers and their workplace suggest they were not able to function as professional educators in some respects, even though in other areas they were. The gap between what they believed and valued, and what they did in their classroom practices was too great to conclude that they were, indeed, well prepared for the complex tasks involved in the daily work of the classroom. The teachers needed more skills and abilities and many more carefully developed opportunities for growth, without which any significant improvement in these schools is doubtful.

The professionalization of the teacher and the conditions of schooling have become a major focus of attention in recent times. Scholars from a variety of perspectives are making clear that the demands and expectations placed upon teachers as professional educators are not adequately supported by their professional preparation or by the school conditions under which they work (Lieberman & Miller, 1984; Lortie, 1975; Wise & Darling-Hammond, 1984/85). The gap between what we would like teachers to do as professional educators and how they are educated, the very low salary scales, the limited opportunities for teachers to continue their professional development, and the restricted conditions under which they work limit their effectiveness and hamper the role that schools can play in our society.

To the degree that your school is like our schools, there is a need for considerable reflection and planning about how your teachers will be encouraged to continue their growth as professional educators over the years. Preservice education provides a foundation for future growth, but it can never produce a completely professional educator. Opportunities for continued professional development must be created and provided, and they must be directly linked to classroom work.

Specifically, your teachers must have many opportunities for continued growth in the specialized skills that are required for them to participate in all the important areas of schooling, including curriculum and instruction, communications with parents, allocation of resources, selection of personnel, and all other areas of faculty concerns. Programs must be offered that are responsive to your teachers' needs and interests; resources must be made available to them in their classrooms; and administrative encouragement must be ever present and clearly evident. Traditional avenues for growth must be continued and made even more effective, and new avenues must be explored.

To accomplish these improvements will be no small task. It will require many resources and much time and dedication. Your teachers must be asked for input and very much involved; outside consultants with varying specializations must be made available; your district personnel and community must be consulted, informed, and involved; and your administrators must be prepared for leadership and assistance to your teachers in curriculum improvement as well as in school management.

Significant changes in your school and curriculum will not occur unless your teachers are encouraged to continue their development as professional educators. Quality education for your students depends upon efforts to assist your teachers to become the best possible professional educators they can be — in the fullest sense of that concept.

CHAPTER 7

Satisfactory and Unsatisfactory Classrooms

Most children enter school at the age of 5 and continue under the direct and powerful influence of a few adults in the elementary school throughout their formative preadolescent years. During this time, students spend approximately 8,000 hours in school as they progress from kindergarten through the sixth grade. These two factors, entrance at an early age and the amount of time spent with a few very influential teachers, mean that the impact of the classroom teacher upon a student's life is likely to be greater at this age than at any other time in the student's schooling. It is essential, then, that you make the elementary school experience for your students the best that is possible.

In this chapter we will take a more detailed look at what daily life in their classrooms was like for the students. We will examine data from a few carefully selected elementary classrooms from the Study of Schooling sample which allow us to "see" them as the students and teachers perceived them. The chapter also represents an example of how you might choose to look more intensively at the data you may have collected for study on topics discussed in the prior chapters. Once you have a data base for examining your school and curriculum, there are a number of ways to use it. While the preceding chapters illustrate the most straightforward way of summarizing and using your raw data, this chapter illustrates a more in-depth way of looking at it. This approach might be used to encourage your teachers to look more critically at their classrooms, in order to determine the quality of daily life at school as their students may be experiencing it. It should also encourage them to think about some fundamental factors that might be involved in establishing the quality of life in their classrooms.

I was intrigued by the differences I could sense in some of the classrooms in our sample. Intuitively, I could tell that some seemed to be "better" than others, and so I decided to pursue the differences by using some of the data already reported and discussed in previous chapters. The basis for selecting the particular sample was the students' views of their classrooms and the experiential curriculum, that is, the perceptions of the students about what they experienced and learned in their classrooms.

The student's view of the classroom is often neglected in educational research. Perceptions of teachers, administrators, observers, and other adults are much more frequently reported. It is the student, however, who is expected to grow and benefit from all the efforts to affect classroom practices. It is the student who personally experiences the daily attempts to provide a good education. Since schooling can be such a powerful factor in a young child's life, an extended look at the student's view of the classroom is very much warranted. You may want to examine your classrooms further, to study questions such as we will explore in this chapter:

- How do your students perceive various aspects of their daily classroom experience?
- Which ones do they like and respond to positively?
- What do they not like about their classrooms?

By necessity, this chapter is somewhat more technical in reporting the data, because it is based on statistical analyses that do not correspond as directly and clearly to the research instruments used in A Study of Schooling as the preceding chapters do. As noted already, however, all the data used in this chapter have been reported elsewhere in the book. While there are no new data in that sense, this chapter examines some data in different ways than have been reported previously. Tables of statistical data are provided to supplement the discussion. By referring to them you will be able to identify clearly the specific items that were basic to this study. The tables also should help you to conduct a similar study of your classrooms, should you want to do a more in-depth investigation.

RATIONALE AND METHODOLOGY

It is clear to anyone who has spent some time in schools and classrooms that there is a sameness to all of them (Goodlad, 1984; Goodlad et al., 1974). A building is immediately identified as a school by its appearance, smells, and sounds. Classrooms are usually the same size, arranged in similar ways, contain familiar materials, and have the same types of people playing similar roles in them. And yet, with all the sameness, there clearly is a difference in the "feel" among classrooms, the quality of life being experienced, and the curriculum being offered and experienced from classroom to classroom.

Classrooms differ in varying ways—sometimes significant and sometimes less important. I was interested in differentiating among good and not-so-good classrooms, as reflected in some of the students' responses to our questionnaires. As the basis of selecting my sample of classrooms, which I ultimately termed satisfactory and unsatisfactory, I identified three significant variables from the research data. They become my bases for differentiation among all the elementary classrooms and thus for selecting a smaller number of both satisfactory and unsatisfactory classrooms for more intensive study. The three variables were

1. The amount of concern the teacher expressed for the student
2. The clarity of the teacher's explanation of learning tasks
3. The extent to which students had some choice in decisions about their learning

I selected these variables because they are important ones in determining the extent to which learning would take place and the quality of daily life in the classrooms. They are essential characteristics of good classrooms for students, in my judgment.

The three variables were then assessed on the basis of scores on selected items from the classroom climate data collected from students, items to which early elementary students were asked to respond with "yes," "sometimes," or "no," and upper elementary students with "usually true" or "usually false." The actual items used are shown in Figure 7.1.

The early and upper elementary student responses for the three variables from each of the classrooms in the sample were then tallied separately and the resulting scores were used to rank-order the classrooms in each group. From the early elementary list, the 12 classrooms with the highest, or most positive, student responses were selected as "satisfactory" classrooms, and the 12 classrooms with the lowest, or least positive, responses were selected as the "unsatisfactory" group. At the upper elementary level, 11 classrooms in each category were similarly identified and selected. Early and upper elementary classrooms were kept separate for data analysis because the questionnaires to which the students responded were slightly different. Although the items had the same intent, they were worded somewhat differently. Also, additional items not in the early elementary student questionnaire were included in the upper elementary one.

Figure 7.1 Items Comprising the Variables Used to Differentiate Satisfactory and Unsatisfactory Classrooms

---

Teacher Concern Scale

Early Elementary Students
My teacher is friendly.
I like my teacher.

Upper Elementary Students
My teacher listens to me.
My teacher makes this class fun for me.
My teacher is friendly.
I like the teacher in this class.
I wish I had a different teacher for
   this class. (-)

Teacher Clarity

Early Elementary Students
I understand what my teacher
   wants me to do.

Upper Elementary Students
Our teacher gives clear directions.

Student Decision Making

Early Elementary Students
I choose what I want to do in this
   class.

Upper Elementary Students
We can choose what we want to
   learn in this class.
I would like more chances to help
   choose what we do in this class.
Students help decide what we do
   in this class.

There was no discernable demographic pattern among the types of schools from which this sample of classrooms was taken. Urban and rural schools, predominantly white and predominantly minority schools, and large and small schools were included in this sample, just as they were in the entire study. In addition, classrooms from the same school appeared in both the satisfactory and unsatisfactory group.

After the satisfactory and unsatisfactory classrooms as defined by the high and low ends of the distribution of student responses on the three selected variables had been identified, I selected other items from the student and teacher questionnaires which I thought reflected important aspects of daily life in the classroom. The purpose of selecting these variables was to identify characteristics of classroom living and learning that might correlate with the level of student satisfaction with the classrooms. Since the teacher, early elementary student, and upper elementary student questionnaires differed in the number and type of questions asked, different items were selected from each questionnaire for further

study. As was the case with the variables used for selecting the classrooms, some of these items had similar intents and others were unique to
the particular questionnaire. Thus, the data we will use to discuss what
the satisfactory and unsatisfactory classrooms looked like from the perspectives of both the teachers and students must be reported separately
for the early elementary and upper elementary levels. Because of the
large number of variables studied, over 500, only those that proved to be
statistically significant are emphasized. Many of the other variables I
selected for study, however, are mentioned, and you will recognize them
as ones we have already discussed in previous chapters.

ASPECTS OF CLASSROOM LIFE FOR
EARLY ELEMENTARY STUDENTS

Student Variables

Forty-five items were selected from the early elementary student
questionnaire for use in determining how the students in the satisfactory
and unsatisfactory classrooms perceived important aspects of daily life
at school. The variables clustered into categories about attitudes toward
school, the curriculum, and self. They also reflected general perceptions
of other students, the teacher, the curriculum, and instruction. Basic
demographics of age and sex of the students were included. Variables
that asked about their attitudes toward school included whether they
wanted to go to a different school, whether they liked doing schoolwork, and whether they liked staying home better than going to school.
Attitudes toward self referred to whether they considered themselves
good readers, whether they were doing the best work they could, and if
they always did what the teacher told them to do. Perceptions of the
teacher asked whether their teacher listened to them, whether their
teacher liked some students better than others, and if the teacher acted
the same toward all students. Perceptions of other students asked if
students helped each other in their class and whether students in class
fought with each other. Variables about instruction were represented by
such items as whether they had enough time to do their work, understood what the teacher wanted them to do, whether the teacher helped
them if they did their work incorrectly, and whether they could choose
what they wanted to do in their class. They were also asked to indicate
which took the most time in their class: passing out materials, learning,
or getting students to behave.

Variables about the curriculum asked the students whether each of the six subject areas — reading/language arts, math, social studies, science, art, and physical education — was "easy," "just right," or "hard" for them. Items were also included that asked whether they liked those same subject areas and liked or disliked some of the typical learning activities in those subject areas.

By far the majority of the items selected did not differentiate between the two groups at a statistically significant level. The 11 items that did significantly differentiate ($p \le .05$) satisfactory and unsatisfactory classrooms are shown in Table 7.1 and discussed here. These 11 items reflected all of the categories of questionnaire items selected for study. More students in grades 1 through 3 from classrooms in the satis-

Table 7.1 Student Variables Differentiating Satisfactory and Unsatisfactory Classrooms: Early Elementary Data

| | Mean Score or % of Students | | |
Variable	Satisfactory Classrooms	Unsatisfactory Classrooms	Significance of Difference
Perceptions of curriculum and instruction			
Is math easy, just right, or hard?[1]	1.56	1.81	**
Do you like reading?[2]	91.1%	81.2%	'
I have enough time to do my work in this class.[3]	2.54	2.29	**
Attitudes toward school and curriculum			
I like to do schoolwork.[3]	2.49	2.17	**
I like school.[3]	2.60	2.27	***
Attitude toward self			
I always do what my teacher tells me to do.[3]	2.85	2.68	**
Perceptions of other students			
The kids in this class help each other.[3]	2.37	2.14	***
Perceptions of the teacher			
My teacher acts the same toward all kids.[3]	2.37	2.03	**
If I do my work wrong, my teacher helps me do it right.[3]	2.34	2.02	*
Demographic variables			
Grade level	1.08	2.12	**
Age	6.42	7.44	***

*$p < .05$ **$p < .01$ ***$p < .001$

[1]Scores for this item were: 1 (easy), 2 (just right), 3 (hard).

[2]Data given represent the percentage of students answering "yes" to this question.

[3]Scores for this item were: 1 (no), 2 (sometimes), 3 (yes).

factory group reported that math was "just right," while in the unsatisfactory classrooms, more students reported math as "hard." A significantly larger percentage of students in classrooms from the satisfactory group than students in the unsatisfactory group reported they liked reading. They reported liking school and schoolwork in general (the curriculum) more often then did students in the unsatisfactory group. Students in the satisfactory group also reported that they complied more often with their teachers' work assignments.

Early elementary students in the satisfactory group reported they more frequently cooperated with or helped each other in the class. Further, they also believed that their teachers more often acted the same toward all students. They also perceived their teachers as being more helpful in teaching them to do their work correctly if they had done it improperly and as providing them with enough time to do the work in their classes. Finally, as shown in Table 7.1, students in classrooms in the satisfactory group were more likely to be at the younger end of our early elementary sample; that is, within ranges of age (6–8 years old) and grade level (Grades 1–3) of the sample, students in satisfactory classrooms were on average 6$^{1/2}$-year-old first graders, whereas those from the unsatisfactory classrooms were 7$^{1/2}$-year-old second graders.

It probably is not surprising that subject areas other than math and reading were not represented among the variables for which there were significant differences between the two groups. Math and reading were by far the most pervasive subject areas in all classrooms, and in many classrooms they were too often the only subject areas emphasized. Throughout the discussions in this book, our data have indicated the greater importance of these two subject areas, relative to the others. Students in these grades had correctly gotten the message as to what part of the curriculum really counts. It is interesting to note that students in the unsatisfactory classrooms already more often perceived math as being harder than did the students in the satisfactory classrooms. Could this be the beginning of math phobia for some students? It is interesting, too, but not surprising, that the overall attitude of students in the satisfactory classrooms was more positive toward reading, school, and schoolwork in general. They perceived their teachers as more often being good instructors, in the sense that their teachers helped them do their work correctly.

It is hard to know how to interpret the findings regarding average age and grade level in the satisfactory and unsatisfactory groups. Our data for the early elementary students seem to suggest that the older the student, the less likely the student's perception of the classroom will place it within the satisfactory group, but there is no similar trend among upper elementary students. It may be that the early elementary students were in fact responding to the increased amount of academic work that typically occurs in second grade, but further study is needed before any solid conclusions can be drawn. If your investigations yield similar results, you might want to examine this hypothesis.

Teacher Variables

The items selected from the elementary teacher questionnaire were divided into the following four parts or topics:

Part 1: Demographics, background, and professional development
Part 2: Perceptions of the school working environment
Part 3: Perceptions of curriculum and instruction, both in general and by subject area
Part 4: Attitudes toward other teachers and the school and toward education in general

Part 1 included such items as age, sex, race and ethnicity, income, political orientation, highest degree held, postcredential work, teaching experience, participation in any professional development activities within the last 3 years, and membership in educational organizations. Part 2 covered teachers' perceptions of their working environment such as whether enough help was available to them, how much control they had over their job and how much they would have liked, and how potential school problems were perceived. Part 3 asked questions such as whether what students were learning was useful to them now and in the future, what functions and goals were emphasized at that school and which ought to be emphasized, teachers' satisfaction with curriculum planning and teaching, their use of behavioral objectives, and how time was spent in their classrooms. Finally, part 4 items asked whether the teachers thought most teachers did a good job in that school and how they graded their school. As with the students, most variables did not differentiate between the satisfactory and unsatisfactory early elementary teachers, but a few did, which suggests that they were very powerful factors in the quality of classroom life.

The classrooms labeled satisfactory on the basis of students' ratings were differentiated from unsatisfactory ones on items from the teacher questionnaire that were arranged into the following five clusters: perceptions of the curriculum in the six subject areas, the control teachers had over some curriculum elements, bases used for individualizing instruction, attitudes toward behavioral objectives, and use of professional resources. These five clusters of items represent only two of the four parts of items from the teacher questionnaire: Part 1, professional development; and part 2, perceptions of curriculum and instruction.

Regarding the first of these five clusters — perceptions of curriculum — one subject area, reading/language arts/English, accounted for all but one of the items that distinguished between the groups of classrooms labeled satisfactory and unsatisfactory at the early elementary level. Social Studies was the only other subject area that was represented. These data are summarized in Table 7.2. As can be seen, compared to those in satisfactory classrooms, the teachers in the unsatisfactory classrooms reported that higher percentages of their students had materials and content in reading/language arts/English that were appropriate to their ethnic or cultural background. The teachers in the satisfactory classrooms, then, perceived more problems with the content and materials, in that they saw them as appropriate for fewer students in relation to their ethnic or cultural backgrounds. Teachers in the group of early elementary classrooms labeled satisfactory reported they found it more useful than the unsatisfactory group to have their students make up their own stories, plays, or poems; and they more often had their students build or draw things and act things out in their English/reading/language arts classes.

For social studies, the only other subject area that had a statistically significant relationship, it was revealed that more teachers in the "satisfactory" classrooms taught that subject in conjunction with other subjects rather than as a separate subject. That is, social studies was taught less as a single, isolated subject during a special time period and more in relation to, or as part of, other subject areas. With the extremely dominant role of reading/language arts in all of the elementary classrooms, we are probably safe in assuming that social studies instruction was related to or a part of the reading/language arts curriculum rather than to any other subject area.

In their perceptions of curriculum and instruction, then, the teachers in "satisfactory" classrooms reported less of a match between the ethnic and cultural backgrounds of their students with English/reading/language arts content and materials; reported more creative, physically overt activities in their classes; and attempted to integrate social studies with other curricula areas — probably with reading/language arts.

The teachers in the satisfactory early elementary classrooms reported they had greater control over setting goals and objectives in their planning and teaching than those in unsatisfactory classrooms. The other curriculum elements of content, learning activities, teaching strategies, materials, evaluation, grouping, time, and space did not differentiate between the two groups on this control variable. However,

Table 7.2 Teacher Variables Differentiating Satisfactory and Unsatisfactory Classrooms: Early Elementary Data

Variable	Mean Score or % of Teachers		Significance of Difference
	Satisfactory Classrooms	Unsatisfactory Classrooms	
Perceptions of Subject-Area Curriculum and Instruction			
Reading/Language Arts/English			
For approximately what percentage of students in this class are the materials and content in this subject appropriate according to the ethnic or cultural background of the students?[1]	3.42	4.45	*
How useful do you think it is to have students make up their own stories, plays or poems?[2]	3.83	3.36	*
How often do students in this class act things out?[2]	2.42	2.00	**
How often do students in this class build or draw things?[2]	3.42	2.64	***
Social Studies			
Do you teach social studies primarily in conjunction with other subjects or as a single subject?[3]	57.1	42.9	*
Perceived Control Over Curricular Elements			
How much control do you feel you have over decisions about setting goals and objectives in your planning and teaching?[1]	4.42	3.83	*
Bases for Individualizing Instruction			
Use of different time schedules for different students.[1]	3.67	2.64	*
Use of different grouping arrangements.[1]	4.18	3.36	*
Use of different activities.[1]	3.73	3.18	*
Use of different content.[1]	3.64	3.00	*
Attitudes Toward Behavioral Objectives			
Behaviorally stated instructional objectives assist me in evaluating student progress.[2]	3.75	3.08	**
Use of Professional Resources			
Indicate whether or not you have consulted district personnel during the last year.[4]	1.75	1.25	**
Indicate how often you have contact with district committees.[5]	1.25	1.67	*

*$p < .05$ **$p < .01$ ***$p < .001$

[1] Scores on this item ranged from 1 (none/almost never/0%) to 5 (all/complete/always/100%)

[2] Scores on this item ranged from 1 (never/not at all/strongly disagree) to 4 (always/very/strongly agree).

[3] Data given represent percentage responding to social studies in conjunction with other subjects.

[4] Scores on this item were: 1 (no), 2 (yes).

[5] Scores on this item were: 1 (never), 2 (occasionally), 3 (fairly often).

four of these curriculum elements did differentiate between the two groups as ways in which teachers individualized their instruction. As can be seen in the table, teachers in the satisfactory classrooms reported the most use of different time schedules for their students, different grouping arrangements, different learning activities, and different content, in order to individualize their instruction. Also, teachers in the satisfactory classrooms reported higher agreement that behavioral objectives assisted them in evaluating student progress than did the teachers in the unsatisfactory classrooms. No benefits of or objections to behavioral objectives, such as assisting students in knowing what they are to learn, helping teachers know what and how to teach, being too simplistic or too time consuming, or being used unfairly to evaluate the teacher, differentiated between the two groups.

There were significant differences, then, between how early elementary teachers in the classrooms labeled satisfactory and unsatisfactory planned for curriculum and instruction. The former believed they had more control over setting their goals and objectives, more often tried to individualize instruction on several curricular elements, and thought behavioral objectives were more useful in helping them to evaluate student progress.

The final cluster of items differentiated between the teachers of the "satisfactory" and "unsatisfactory" classrooms on the basis of professional development. More teachers in the satisfactory early elementary classrooms had consulted district personnel during the last year, but they also reported less professional work with district committees than did teachers in the unsatisfactory ones. It may be that consultants were helpful to them in curriculum planning but that committee work was a distraction from doing the important curriculum work that distinguished their classrooms. Should you find similar data, your teachers might consider asserting their power over curriculum planning more than the average teacher in this study seemed to, by being creative in planning classroom activities and using district personnel as consultants frequently, but avoiding district committee work.

ASPECTS OF CLASSROOM LIFE FOR UPPER ELEMENTARY STUDENTS

Student Variables

Over 200 variables were selected for further study from the upper elementary student questionnaire. They included items dealing with attitudes toward school, curriculum, other students, and self. Items regarding attitudes toward school asked whether they thought their school was safe and what they saw as the most important aspect of schooling. Items on attitudes toward self asked whether they felt good about the class, if they did better than other students, if they knew what to do in the class, and if they cared about what they were expected to do. Questions about curriculum and instruction included their perceptions of the importance of each of the six subject areas and whether they liked those subject areas; how time was spent in their classrooms; and about activities, materials, and grouping patterns within the six subject areas. Also included were variables that asked about their perceptions of the teacher, classroom life, future plans, curriculum, and instruction.

Items from upper elementary school students that significantly differentiated between satisfactory and unsatisfactory classrooms were clustered in four major areas: perceptions about curriculum and instruction, attitudes toward other students, attitudes toward school and schoolwork in general (curriculum), and perceptions of the teacher. Table 7.3 shows the specific items that were statistically significant.

As with the early elementary students, the subject area of reading/language arts/English was the one that most often differentiated between the two groups of classrooms. Compared to students in the unsatisfactory classrooms, those in the satisfactory ones reported greater use of materials other than just the text, such as films, filmstrips, slides, games, tapes, and records. More of them also liked to use games in their reading/language arts/English classes. More liked to remember facts, dates, words, names, or rules — a low-level cognitive activity. At first, it may be surprising to you that those items reflecting higher cognitive activities did not differentiate between the two types of classrooms. Based upon our other data, including the observation data reported on in chapter 3, however, there were not many higher-level cognitive activities offered in any of the classrooms. Therefore there was no basis for differentiation on those factors.

Other activities that more students in the satisfactory classrooms reported they liked in reading/language arts/English classes were listening to the teacher, having class discussions, and acting things out. Not only did more of them like these activities, they also reported they actually did these activities more frequently; and more of them built or drew things, wrote answers to questions, and read for fun more often, although their liking for these latter three activities was about the same as the unsatisfactory classrooms. The students in the satisfactory classrooms rated reading/language arts/English as more interesting to them than those in the unsatisfactory classrooms. Finally, far fewer students

(text continues on p. 160)

Table 7.3 Student Variables Differentiating Satisfactory and Unsatisfactory Classrooms: Upper Elementary Data

Variable	Mean Score or % of Students		Significance of Difference
	Satisfactory Classrooms	Unsatisfactory Classrooms	
Perceptions of Curriculum and Instruction			
Reading/Language Arts/English			
Do you usually like to use games in this class?[1]	94.2%	84.1%	*
Do you use in this class:			
Films, filmstrips, or slides?[1]	86.9%	64.6%	*
Games?[1]	74.8%	50.3%	*
Tape recordings or records?[1]	70.1%	48.6%	*
Do you usually like to remember facts, dates, words, names, or rules?[1]	67.1%	49.9%	**
Do you usually like to:			
Listen to the teacher when he/she talks or shows how to do something?[1]	88.4%	70.6%	**
Have class discussions?[1]	70.9%	55.1%	**
Act things out?[1]	74.6%	62.6%	**
Do you in this class:			
Listen to the teacher when he/she talks or shows how to do something?[1]	96.7%	89.3%	*
Have class discussions?[1]	82.0%	64.8%	*
Build or draw things?[1]	79.9%	57.1%	**
Write answers to questions?[1]	92.6%	84.2%	*
Act things out?[1]	58.0%	37.5%	*
Read for fun?[1]	85.2%	71.6%	**
How often can you choose your own books and materials in this class?[2]	27.6%	47.8%	**
How interesting for you is [this class]?[3]	3.20	2.82	*
Social Studies			
In general, how important is [this class]?[3]	3.55	3.30	*
How interesting for you is [this class]?[3]	3.04	2.69	
Science			
How interesting for you is [this class]?[3]	3.89	3.09	*
Instruction			
In this class, how much time is usually taken by:			
Getting students to behave[4]	1.87	2.23	***
Daily routines[4]	1.69	1.53	*
The grades or marks I get in this class are fair.[5]	1.88	1.73	***
We have to learn things without knowing why.[5]	1.29	1.48	***
If I do my work wrong my teacher tells me how to do it right.[5]	1.91	1.70	***
Our teacher tells us ahead of time what we are going to be learning about.[5]	1.75	1.61	***
I do all the work my teacher gives me.[5]	1.87	1.76	**
I do not have enough time to do my work for this class.[5]	1.23	1.43	***
I forget things I've been taught in this class because I don't practice them enough.[5]	1.31	1.41	*
Our teacher never changes his/her mind about anything.[5]	1.35	1.49	*

Variable	Mean Score or % of Students		Significance of Difference
	Satisfactory Classrooms	Unsatisfactory Classrooms	
Attitudes Toward Other Students			
Students in this class yell at each other.[5]	1.43	1.69	***
Students don't care about what goes on in this class.[5]	1.31	1.54	***
Many students don't know what they're supposed to be doing during class.[5]	1.47	1.68	***
Peer Esteem Scale[7]	1.85	1.73	***
Attitudes Toward School and Schoolwork in General (curriculum)			
There are places in this school where I don't go because I'm afraid of other students.[1]	56.6%	75.7%	**
There are not enough materials for everyone in this class to use.[5]	1.26	1.47	**
If you had to choose the one most important thing for you, which of [these] would it be?			
To get a good job[1]	16.2%	27.8%	*
To become a better person[1]	22.9%	14.3%	*
Which one of [these] does the school think is the most important thing for students?			
To get a good job[1]	9.5%	17.5%	*
What grade would you give this school?[6]	4.23	3.58	**
I feel good about what happens in this class.[5]	1.84	1.50	***
I like the way this classroom looks.[5]	1.92	1.62	***
Perceptions of the Teacher			
Teacher Punitive Scale[8]	1.10	1.29	***
The teacher likes some students in this class better than others.[5]	1.40	1.69	***
Our teacher has fun teaching this class.[5]	1.91	1.53	***
Our teacher treats us like babies.[5]	1.09	1.38	***
Many teachers at this school don't care about students.[1]	47.0%	70.3%	**

$^*p < .05$ $^{**}p < .01$ $^{***}p < .001$

[1]Percentage of students responding "usually true."

[2]Percentage of students responding "never."

[3]Scores on this item ranged from 1 (very unimportant/uninteresting) to 4 (very important/interesting).

[4]Scores on this item, which was a 3-item forced choice, were: 1 (least), 2 (next most), 3 (most).

[5]Scores on this item were: 1 (usually false), 2 (usually true).

[6]Scores on this item ranged from 5 ("A") to 1 ("F").

[7]This scale is a composite score of responses to the following five statements: "Students in this class are unfriendly to me. I like working with other students in this class. I like my classmates. In this class, people care about me. My classmates like me." Except for the first question, where scoring was reversed, scores on these items were usually true (2) or usually false (1).

[8]This scale is a composite score of responses to the following five statements: "My teacher hurts my feelings. I'm afraid of my teacher. My teacher gets mad when I ask a question. My teacher makes fun of me. My teacher punishes me unfairly." Scores on these items were usually true (2) or usually false (1).

in the satisfactory classrooms reported that they never had the opportunity to choose their learning materials in this subject area.

In social studies classes, as shown in Table 7.3, more students in the satisfactory classrooms than in the unsatisfactory classrooms reported that they considered social studies as very important and interesting to them. More students in the satisfactory classrooms also reported they found science interesting. Other subject areas did not differentiate between the groups of classrooms, on either importance or interest.

In the area of instruction, the two types of classrooms differed with regard to which of three kinds of activities — getting students to behave, daily routines, and learning — were the most and least time consuming. Although specific amounts of time were not indicated, students in the unsatisfactory classrooms more often saw behavior control as the primary activity than did students in the satisfactory classrooms. The latter group, meanwhile, more often chose daily routines as the most time-consuming classroom activity. The groups were not significantly different in their rating of time spent on instruction, however. Perhaps the daily routines attended to in the satisfactory classrooms contributed to a more comfortable, predictable place for students to be.

Students in the unsatisfactory classrooms more frequently reported that they had to learn things without knowing why, that they did not have enough time to do their work, that they forgot things they had been taught because they did not practice them enough, and that their teacher never changed his or her mind about anything. By contrast, students in the satisfactory classrooms more frequently reported that the grades they received were fair, that their teacher would help them if they did their work incorrectly, that their teacher told them ahead of time what they would be learning about, and that they did all the work their teacher gave them.

Through student perceptions, then, the teachers in the unsatisfactory classrooms tended less often to be clear about instructional purposes, to provide enough time or practice for learning tasks, and to be flexible. Teachers in the satisfactory classrooms, on the other hand, tended more often to be fair in the grades they gave, to be helpful in the learning process, to be clear about what was to be studied, and to have students who did the work given them. It should not be difficult to select with which of these two samples of teachers your students might choose to spend their school days. The results on these variables emphasize the importance of the instructional skill of the teacher in the perceptions of students.

The second cluster of items on which the two groups of classrooms differentiated centered on attitudes toward other students. Referring once more to Table 7.3, it can be seen that students in the satisfactory upper elementary classrooms had the more positive overall perceptions of other students in their classes, as measured by the Peer Esteem Scale. This scale had items dealing with how friendly other students were, whether individual students liked their classmates, whether their classmates liked them, whether people cared about them, and whether they liked working with other students in the class. A contrast can be seen on some of the other variables included in this cluster. In particular, more students in the unsatisfactory classrooms reported that students yelled at each other and did not care about what went on in the class. Thus, classroom dissonance among students appeared to be a characteristic more prevalent in the unsatisfactory classrooms in this sample, while students were perceived to be friendlier in the satisfactory classrooms.

The third cluster of variables that differentiated between the two groups of classrooms was attitudes toward school and schoolwork in general (the curriculum). Students in the satisfactory classrooms gave their schools an average grade of B, compared to the C$^+$ given to their schools by students in the unsatisfactory classrooms. Students also were asked to select the one most important thing that the school had to teach them as individual students — from among the four goals of (1) working well with other people; (2) learning the basic skills in reading, writing, arithmetic, and other important subjects; (3) becoming a better person; or (4) getting a good job. These two groups both chose the second goal the most often and were not significantly different on this point. There were differences between the two groups, however, on the third and fourth goals. More students in the unsatisfactory classrooms than in the satisfactory ones chose the goal of getting a good job, while more students in the satisfactory classrooms selected the goal of becoming a better person. The students in the unsatisfactory classrooms were also more likely than those in satisfactory ones to believe that the school itself placed the most emphasis on preparing its students to get good jobs.

More students in the unsatisfactory classrooms said there were places in the school where they would not go because they were afraid of other students. More also reported there were not enough materials for the students in their classes. By contrast, more students in the satisfactory classrooms than in the unsatisfactory ones reported that they felt good about what happened in their classes and that they liked the way their classroom looked.

The final cluster of upper elementary student variables differentiating between the two samples of classrooms was student perception of the teacher. A scale measuring the punitiveness of the teacher was used, as well as various single items about other student opinions. Referring again to Table 7.3, we can see that, overall, students in the unsatisfactory classrooms reported their teachers were more punitive than did the students in the satisfactory ones. In addition, they more frequently believed that their teacher liked some students better than others, that their teacher treated them like babies, and that many teachers at their school did not care about students. By contrast, more students in the satisfactory classrooms reported that their teacher had fun teaching their class.

Should you find that the classrooms at your school reflect some of the more negative tendencies identified by these data, efforts should be devoted to improving the conditions that your students perceive as being so negative. If some of your students see their teacher in such an undesirable way, school cannot be a very pleasant place for them to be. They could be learning some very powerful, negative messages from the implicit curriculum in their classrooms. Student perceptions of the teacher deserve very special consideration as a part of your curriculum improvement plan.

Teacher Variables

Most of the same variables were selected for study from the upper elementary teacher questionnaires as were used from the early elementary teacher questionnaires. The group of variables that differentiated between satisfactory and unsatisfactory upper elementary classrooms from the teacher questionnaires clustered into three areas: perceptions of subject-area curriculum and instruction, attitudes toward school, and professional background. Items about perceptions of curriculum and instruction included attitudes toward the six subject areas, and toward the following nonsubject-specific aspects: perceived usefulness of what students learned, amount of control over curriculum elements, satisfaction with curriculum elements, and bases for individualizing instruction. The second cluster of attitudes toward school included grades given to the school by its teachers and perceived problems at the school. Finally, the third cluster had to do with the use of professional resources.

As shown in Table 7.4, the only curriculum area that differentiated between the two groups of classrooms was reading/language arts/English, with several items showing significant differences. Teachers in the satisfactory classrooms believed more strongly in the usefulness of having students listen when they were talking or demonstrating how to do something, compared to teachers in the unsatisfactory classrooms. Undoubtedly this is a factor in obtaining and keeping students' attention during the learning process. Perhaps teachers who believed that what they were saying to students was important were the most likely to insist that students be quiet and listen. Teachers in the satisfactory classrooms also reported using games and simulations more often than teachers in unsatisfactory ones. They perceived the materials and content they used to be appropriate for more of their students in terms of their interests and ability level. In general, then, the teachers in the satisfactory classrooms seemed to be more effective in making curriculum and instruction in reading/language arts/English more appropriate and interesting for their students.

Of 11 potential sources of influence over what teachers taught, only one differentiated between the two groups. Teachers in the unsatisfactory classrooms reported that teachers' unions had a greater influence on what they taught in this subject area than the teachers in the satisfactory classrooms did. It would be very interesting to know more about this relationship. If this means that teachers in the less satisfactory classrooms were more in touch with the resources of the teachers' union than those teachers with satisfactory classrooms, it may have been because the former felt less secure in their jobs for some reason. Our data did not address why this relationship occurred, but it would be interesting for you to pursue, should you find a similar relationship.

Teachers in the satisfactory classrooms believed more strongly than those in unsatisfactory ones that what their students were learning in general was relevant for what they needed to know, both for the present and for later in their lives. Thus, relevancy of content being taught was perceived more positively by teachers in the satisfactory classrooms on this general dimension as well as for specific content taught and materials used in the most significant curriculum area of reading/language arts/English.

Compared to the teachers in unsatisfactory classrooms, teachers in the satisfactory classrooms reported more control over the curriculum element of grouping students for instruction. This element is clearly one over which all teachers would be expected to have great, if not complete, control. The lower scores among the teachers in the unsatisfactory classrooms may simply mean that they did not use instructional groups as much.

Three more curriculum elements differentiated between the two types of classrooms when teachers were asked how satisfied they were with these elements. Teachers in the satisfactory classrooms expressed greater satisfaction with their selection of learning activities, teaching techniques, and scheduling of time. However decisions about these curriculum elements were being made, the teachers were quite satisfied

Table 7.4 Teacher Variables Differentiating Satisfactory and Unsatisfactory Classrooms: Upper Elementary Data

Variable	Mean Score		Significance of Difference
	Satisfactory Classrooms	Unsatisfactory Classrooms	
Perceptions of Curriculum and Instruction			
Reading/Language Arts/English			
How useful do you think [it] is or would be for students learning in this subject [to]: Listen to me when I talk or demonstrate how to do something?[1]	3.89	3.44	*
How often is each thing used in this class? Games or simulations[1]	2.78	1.89	**
Learning kits[1]	2.67	1.78	*
For approximately what [proportion] of students in this class are the materials and content in this subject appropriate, according to . . . the following criteria? Interests of the students[2]	4.11	2.89	*
Ability level of student[2]	4.44	3.56	*
How much influence does . . . the following have on what you teach in this subject? Teachers' Union[1]	1.0	1.56	*
Perceived Usefulness of What Students Learn			
What students are learning in this school will be useful for what they need to know NOW.[1]	3.50	3.10	*
What students are learning in this school will be useful for what they need to know LATER in life.[1]	3.35	3.00	*
Perceived Control Over Curricular Elements			
How much control do you feel you have over decisions about: Grouping students for instruction[2]	4.64	4.00	*
Satisfaction with Curricular Elements			
How satisfied are you with: Selecting learning activities[1]	3.55	2.89	*
Selecting teaching techniques[1]	3.64	2.88	*
Scheduling time use[1]	3.73	2.67	*
Bases for Individualizing Instruction			
How frequently do you utilize [this factor] if and when you individualize instruction? Student preferences[1]	2.82	2.11	*
Attitude Toward School			
Students are often given the grades [A-F] to describe the quality of their work. If schools could be graded in the same way, what grade would you give this school?[3]	4.27	3.33	*

Table 7.4, *continued*

| Variable | Mean Score | | Significance of Difference |
	Satisfactory Classrooms	Unsatisfactory Classrooms	
Perceived Problems at the School			
Indicate the extent to which you think [this] is a problem at this school.[4]			
Student misbehavior	2.00	2.60	*
Professional Background			
Indicate whether you consulted with district personnel during the last year.[5]	1.67	1.20	*
How much do educational organizations affect your working conditions?[1]	1.70	2.70	*

*$p < .05$ **$p < .01$

[1]Scores on this item ranged from 1 (never/none/not at all/strongly disagree) to 4 (almost always/a lot/very much/strongly agree).

[2]Scores on this item ranged from 1 (none/not at all) to 5 (all/complete)

[3]Scores on this item ranged from 5 ("A") to 1 ("F").

[4]Scores on this item were: 1 (not a problem), 2 (minor problem), 3 (major problem).

[5]Scores on this item were: 1 (no), 2 (yes).

with the results. Also, they more often considered student preferences as one type of information they used when individualizing instruction.

In the second cluster of variables — attitudes toward school — teachers in the satisfactory classrooms graded their school higher on the average (a grade of B) than did the teachers in the unsatisfactory ones (a grade of C). In addition, teachers in the unsatisfactory classrooms perceived student misbehavior as a more serious problem than the teachers in the satisfactory ones. Overall, however, they did not perceive it as a problem. Perhaps the lack of instructional skills of the teachers in the unsatisfactory classrooms contributed to the minor problems they had with student misbehavior.

Finally, in the third cluster of variables, more of the teachers in the satisfactory classrooms than the unsatisfactory ones had consulted with district personnel during the last year, while the teachers in the unsatisfactory classrooms indicated that educational organizations had a greater impact on their working conditions. It would be interesting to know whether the union figured prominently among these educational organizations. From the other evidence presented, it seems that this is possible.

Once again, the importance of district personnel to teachers in the satisfactory classrooms appears. Although overall our elementary teachers in the Study of Schooling indicated that district personnel were not very influential sources of what they taught, for this smaller sample of teachers in satisfactory upper elementary school classrooms, district personnel were important. Perhaps the problem was not so much what district personnel could do, but rather how to make them available to do more for and work more closely with the classroom teachers.

TOWARD A DEFINITION OF SATISFACTORY CLASSROOMS

The perceptions of the respondents on the majority of over 500 variables from the early and upper elementary student and teacher questionnaires selected for further study were not statistically significant in differentiating between what I have labeled the satisfactory and unsatisfactory classrooms. In most respects, then, teachers and students viewed their classrooms quite similarly. There were some variables, as we have seen, that did significantly differentiate between the two types of classrooms, and they proved to be pervasive and powerful ones in describing the differences between the two groups in the teaching and learning processes and the quality of life in the classrooms. These variables included some of the professional skills of the teachers in curriculum and instruction, attitudes toward the teacher and other students, and perceptions of self. The following summary of the significant variables begins to define what these students' perceptions led me to label as satisfactory classrooms. These variables should help direct your discussions of what a good classroom is, as you study the classrooms in your school.

Perceptions of the curriculum, particularly those of reading/language arts/English, formed a major category differentiating between the two groups of classrooms. In the satisfactory classrooms, at the early elementary level the use of nontraditional, physical, creative activities was more frequent, and at the upper elementary level supplementary resources such as audiovisual materials, games, and stimulations were used more frequently. In the upper elementary satisfactory classrooms, even the more traditional classroom activities such as listening to the teacher, engaging in class discussions, and writing answers to questions were reported by students with greater frequency than in the unsatisfactory classrooms.

The teachers in the early elementary satisfactory classrooms reported that materials and content were inappropriate for a higher percentage of their students, according to their ethnic or cultural backgrounds, than in the unsatisfactory classrooms. By the time the students had reached the upper grades, ethnicity had ceased to be a significant factor; however, the materials and content were reported by teachers in the satisfactory classrooms to be appropriate for more of their students, according to their abilities and interests. Teachers in the upper elementary satisfactory classrooms believed more strongly than those in unsatisfactory ones that what the students were learning was important to them, both for the present and for the future. Reading/language arts/English and science were more interesting to the upper elementary students in satisfactory classrooms than to students in unsatisfactory classrooms, and social studies was perceived as more important. Fewer students in upper elementary satisfactory classrooms reported that they never had the opportunity to choose their materials in reading/language arts/English.

It is interesting that reading/language arts/English was the only subject area that consistently differentiated between the two groups of classrooms. This raises some important questions which you might pursue with your teachers should you find a similar pattern.

- Is the curriculum so imbalanced that reading/language arts/English is essentially *the* curriculum for your school?
- Are the other curriculum areas taught so infrequently or incompletely that your students clearly get the message that what really matters in the elementary school curriculum is only reading/language arts/English?

Some of our evidence suggested the answer to these questions was yes for our schools.

The predominance of this subject area might have occurred for several reasons. Perhaps the teachers in the satisfactory classrooms were just unusually skilled in that subject area. It might also have been because more of them majored in it in college or had done inservice work in it. Yet another explanation might have been that the other subject areas, when they were taught, resembled reading/language arts/English so much that students had a hard time differentiating among some of the subjects. This explanation is not so clearly supported by our data, but it does reflect the reality of the elementary school classroom, which must respond to strong societal pressures to have good standardized test scores in reading and math. The latter would have been easily separated from other subject areas, but social studies and science might simply have been another lesson in reading and writing for many of these students. If such a condition exists at your school, the question you could raise is what your students are missing by not having a strong social studies and science curriculum. Having only reading/language arts/English as the curriculum emphasis in those two subject areas neglects the full range of learning students could gain from them. If this condition exists at your school, do you want it to be so?

In the "satisfactory" classrooms, the teachers reported considerable personal control over setting goals and objectives at the early elementary level and over the grouping of students at the upper elementary level; at both levels they expressed greater satisfaction with their planning and teaching of some curricular elements, namely, learning activities, teaching techniques, and time. Teachers in the satisfactory early-level classrooms more frequently individualized the work of students through the use of such different curriculum elements as time schedules, grouping patterns, activities, and content; and teachers in the satisfactory upper elementary classrooms reported consideration of student preferences more often as a basis for individualizing instruction. Early elementary teachers in satisfactory classrooms agreed more strongly than the others that behavioral objectives helped them evaluate student learning. More teachers in the satisfactory classrooms at both levels also had consulted district personnel during the past year, and those at the early level reported less contact with district committees than the teachers in unsatisfactory classrooms.

Instructional skills of the teachers also differentiated between the satisfactory and unsatisfactory classrooms. Students in the satisfactory classrooms at one or both levels perceived their teachers as more often telling them why they had to do their work and what they would be doing in advance, helping them do their work correctly, providing adequate time and practice, having work at an appropriate level, and grading them fairly. At the same time, these students reported that they more frequently complied with their teachers' expectations for them to do their work.

The instructional skills of teachers that significantly differentiated between the two groups of classrooms, however, reflected primarily only one approach — the direct teaching model. This was without question due primarily to the fact that most of the questionnaire items were written from this perspective. A few were not, however, such as students having some choice in selecting their materials, but these other variables did not consistently differentiate between the two groups of classrooms. Only those skills related to direct instruction separated out the two groups of classrooms. Clearly, the teachers in the satisfactory classrooms were skilled in direct instruction.

While there is no doubt that the direct teaching model is essential for many types of learning that your students are expected to achieve, it certainly has its limitations and cannot help your students achieve other important goals as effectively as other teaching strategies. Your teachers must have the necessary skills in alternative teaching models to help their students achieve the diverse outcomes of a balanced curriculum, if that is what you desire. The current emphasis on helping teachers develop skills only in direct instruction means that you will need to devote more effort toward helping your teachers develop skills in a variety of strategies (Joyce & Weil, 1985). Using only one teaching approach will create an imbalanced curriculum just as surely as teaching only one subject area.

Some of the variables that differentiated between the two groups of classrooms were affective in nature, relating to attitudes and classroom climate. They were undoubtedly powerful elements of the implicit curriculum for this sample of students, teaching them important lessons about their capabilities as students, about what teachers and peers were like, and about the schooling process. One of these affective clusters was attitude toward school. Students in the satisfactory early elementary classrooms reported greater liking of school and schoolwork than did those in unsatisfactory classrooms, and students at the upper level graded their schools higher. Compared to students in the unsatisfactory classrooms, they also perceived the school to be a safer, more attractive place for them and felt better about what happened in their classrooms.

Another cluster of affective variables centered on student attitudes toward their peers and teachers, such as perceptions of their classmates as friendly and their teachers as fair and helpful. Students in the satisfactory early-level classrooms more frequently said their classmates helped each other and at the upper level more often liked the way their classroom looked and felt. The teachers in the satisfactory classrooms at one or both levels were perceived as being friendlier, more enthusiastic, fairer to all students, and less punitive than the teachers in the unsatisfactory classrooms. Further, these teachers seemed to pay more attention to the personal function of schooling and to individual students. By contrast, the unsatisfactory classrooms at one or both levels, according to the students, had more dissonance among students and had teachers who were more punitive and more often treated students like babies, liked some students more than others, and were inflexible.

The satisfactory teacher, then, might be tentatively defined as a person who is friendly, enthusiastic, caring, and supportive, and who possesses essential professional skills for teaching effectively and making subjects interesting. Both personal and professional characteristics thus define the effective teacher, from the students' perspectives. This type of teacher undoubtedly has a profound effect upon the experiential curriculum of your students.

You must not underestimate the importance of these factors in beginning to define satisfactory classrooms and satisfactory teachers in regard to the quality of life for students in your elementary school. The interactions among teachers and students in your classrooms have a tremendous impact upon how students view their life at school. The data in this chapter highlight the importance of not only the professional skills of the teacher but also the affective variables involved in creating good relationships in the daily life of the classroom.

It is essential, then, that you help your teachers to gain not only the necessary professional skills in curriculum and instruction but also the interpersonal skills they need to work with students in friendly, personal, interested, fair, caring, comfortable ways. Your teachers must be able to conduct life in the classroom in an organized way that facilitates learning for the students and helps students enjoy being there. Too often research findings emphasize teachers' skills in direct instruction and very much neglect these more affective characteristics of the classroom. This study strongly suggests that it cannot be an either/or condition for the students. For your school to be a comfortable and productive place in which your students can learn and experience quality schooling, your teachers must be prepared both to teach students and to relate to them socially and personally.

You may ultimately want to include in your program of curriculum improvement all of the many variables that differentiated between satisfactory and unsatisfactory classrooms in our sample. All of them need to receive increased attention from researchers and practitioners in programs for continuing the professional development of teachers. The difficulties of working on the problems in the affective and interpersonal domains increase the challenge of this task, but it is nonetheless just as essential. Your teachers must be able to relate well to their students *and* teach them effectively, if your school is to be a satisfactory place for your students to be.

CHAPTER 8

A Look to the Future

We are engaged in this country in an intense period of school and curriculum reform. We are hit from all sides with demands for curriculum improvement. Public opinion polls indicate the majority of the lay public believes that the schools have limitations that must be addressed. Research studies document the gap between what the schools are expected to do and what goes on inside the classrooms. Commission after commission at the state and federal levels cite the need for reform and make pronouncements as to what changes ought to occur and how they should be accomplished. Prestigious professional educators and lay citizens form study groups and formulate what they believe should be done to change the schools. No one can escape the pervasive message that our schools are in need of improvement.

But these suggestions and demands are not dramatically different from some past attempts at reform. Such efforts seem to come and go in American education with predictable frequency. Specifics may change on what needs to be improved; old ideas may be tested once again and either kept or discarded, according to their usefulness for the evolving demands placed on the elementary school; new ideas will be advocated for inclusion into the intended curriculum and classroom practices; and new programs will be proposed to help teachers become more effective professional educators. Even after these have been dealt with, calls for reform will come again in the future.

Schools have responded to the current reform initiatives in a variety of ways—thoughtfully, hurriedly, or superficially. Some have simply gone on conducting school as they had in the past. The current round of school reform may be abating somewhat as schools herald their successes, proudly announcing higher test scores, more students in science and math courses, more rigorous courses for all students, increased standards for all students, more required homework, and more emphasis throughout the curriculum on higher cognitive skills.

At the same time, we may already be seeing the beginning of another reform period, with the growing concern about dropouts, the extended view of what literacy means, the concern for AIDS, and in-

171

creased discussions about the importance of the local school in reform efforts. Perhaps rather than being threatened by or cynical about these repeated calls for reforms, we should welcome and expect them in our roles as professional educators. They may well reflect the fundamental role our schools play in this nation. We dare not allow our schools to drift aimlessly as we complacently maintain the status quo at school and turn blind eyes to the changing society around us. Our schools must change with the times and keep abreast of the new demands of living in our world. The old adage that nothing is assured in life but change may as accurately describe the conditions of schooling as it does other areas of life.

In any reform initiative, the local school is where many decisions must ultimately be made about how the school will change, if at all. All the pressures for change from the various sources must be considered, of course, but school and curriculum reform will not be conducted at the national, state, or district level with much effectiveness unless the faculty of the individual school agrees with, accepts, and diligently works for any given expectation for improvement. Curriculum reform must be based upon a careful and systematic process of study and deliberation of what your school is like now and what you would like it to be. Reform will come through your attempts to make those two factors in school improvement as similar as possible. That is what this book is about.

Without a knowledge of what your school is like and how your faculty would like it to change, it is impossible to develop a systematic, informed program for curriculum improvement. Without an examination of the issues and implications related to the changes proposed for curriculum improvement, changes may well occur simply for the sake of change, and they could create unanticipated, perhaps even worse, problems in the future. To subscribe blindly to the reform proposals of others is to be hostage to the vision and expectations of someone else.

GUIDELINES FOR CURRICULUM REFORM

The purpose of this final chapter is to make some recommendations that might help you cope with the continual calls for curriculum reform. As you engage in your current program for curriculum improvement, perhaps based in part upon some ideas in this book, you may well have to consider new demands, ideas, and expectations from a variety of diverse groups and pressures. But through your ongoing efforts for curriculum improvement, the process of articulating what your vision is of good schooling and how that vision can be made a reality should become a way of life for your faculty. The new expectations and calls for reform can then be considered in relation to a continual process rather than be seen as entirely new. Over time, a deliberate, systematic, ongoing approach to curriculum improvement will evolve into a process with which you will be comfortable and which will serve you well as specific demands for curriculum reform come and go.

Regardless of the amount of resources you expend this year on curriculum improvement, there will be tasks that remain to be done in the future. To help you cope with this fact, the following eight recommendations are offered. They do not tell you specifically what you ought to do but suggest a broad way of viewing and managing your curriculum improvement efforts so that you will be prepared to examine for yourself any future proposal for reform. The recommendations emphasize the importance of continuing to create your own agenda in the future and of developing the ability and confidence you need to implement it. The recommendations should remind you of the importance of the task you are undertaking, give you the confidence to continue the study of your school, and suggest some ideas to make your work easier.

1. *Approach curriculum improvement as an ongoing task.* Do not expect ever to be really through with it. A good curriculum is always evolving, since knowledge, conditions, society, teachers, students, administrators, and parents change. As the social and school contexts within which your curriculum is offered change, it, too, must change. But take heart — what you did yesterday or are doing today to improve your curriculum is part of a process you can use for tomorrow. The process of inquiry into what your curriculum is like now and what you want it to be can be used again and again — no matter what the specifics of the latest reform may be. The process of inquiry will become second nature to you, and through it you will be better equipped to conduct future reforms.

2. *Keep a broad view of what your school can do for your students and our society.* Do not be intimidated by powerful arguments for restricting the mission of the elementary school to only a part of what you may feel it can do for your students. Keep a clear vision of what you think schooling ought to be like, even though it, too, will need to be revised as conditions change. Share your vision with all those who have a concern for your school, and listen to them as they share theirs with you. Out of such discussions should come a common vision toward which all those concerned with your school can work to make it a reality.

3. *Always be on the lookout for resources that can help you improve your curriculum.* Go to conferences and staff development programs, read professional publications regularly, confer with district and

county consultants about the latest ideas in curriculum and instruction, talk with your communities and parents about their hopes and expectations for your school, lobby with public officials for financial support on behalf of your faculty and students, and contact university professors about their research and proposals about making schools better places for living and learning. Be willing to commit your scarce resources to helping your faculty continue to grow as professional educators. Time for reflection and sharing, ideas to consider, money to buy whatever is essential, people who want to grow and change, and dedication to the importance of curriculum in the lives of your students are necessary resources that you must garner from wherever they are available.

4. *Expect your attempts at change to take time and occur in small steps.* Improving your school will not occur in a short period of time. You will have to support and reassure teachers who are struggling with new ideas, parents who are fearful that their children will not get the best education possible if too many changes are made, and a system that is going to continue as it has been unless considerable effort is expended to make it change. As recommended in chapter 1, begin with a small part of the curriculum that you want to change, work with it until it approaches what you want, and then select another aspect to work on, making sure to revisit periodically what you have already accomplished. Through such a process the enormous task of curriculum improvement is made manageable and you will not be overwhelmed by all that must be done. With dedication and persistence, desired changes can be made over time.

5. *Maximize in every possible way the continued growth and professionalization of your teachers.* The significant role that teachers play in the lives of their students must never be neglected or forgotten. It is they who must ultimately improve the education of your students. Encourage your teachers to grow and develop through examining what they are doing and why; help them locate, analyze, and experiment with good ideas; support them in their faltering attempts at change; help soothe their guilt over mistakes and failures; and take time to celebrate their successes. Have faith in the power of your staff to select and implement good ideas, develop a vision, locate resources, resolve problems, and design successful classroom practices for the kind of curriculum wanted at your school. Inquiry into these tasks of curriculum improvement help, in part, to define the professional teacher we so desperately need in our schools today.

6. *Consistently monitor your vision of what ought to be, your intended curriculum, and the practices of your school.* Monitor your vision and practices in relation to what has been traditionally done at

your school. Challenge practices and conditions that are maintained just for the sake of tradition—uninformed protection of the way things have always been does not serve us well in today's world. Monitor your vision and practices, too, in relation to the changes that are occurring throughout the nation and world. Try to identify the problems and achievements that are going to affect the teachers and students in your elementary school. Stay abreast of scientific, technological, political, social, and physical changes wherever they occur. Any of them may have great potential impact upon the curriculum of your elementary school. It is not enough that you identify them; you must decide how to respond to them and when. It may be necessary to be proactive in your thinking rather than reactive; that is, you may decide to change an aspect of the curriculum before a new commission can be appointed to study a problem and recommend what they believe should be done.

7. *Adopt a spirit of inquiry, as encouraged in this book, and work to make it become a pervasive characteristic of your school.* Encourage your staff to use inquiry not only for developing your program of curriculum improvement, but also for interacting with other staff members, parents, district and state educators, consultants, and the lay communities. Support your faculty in consistently demonstrating their willingness to search for answers, their awareness of the frequent necessity of taking action in the real world of schooling before definitive answers can be provided, and their willingness to reexamine a decision as new data become available. Openness to alternative ideas, the ability for critical examination of and reflection about the issues imbedded within proposals for improvement, and commitment to the best school program for your students should become major characteristics of your faculty in every educational setting.

8. *Be aware of the continued need to consider the expectations and involvement of others in curriculum improvement processes.* Your faculty, no matter how important they are in the daily life of your school, are not the only participants in curriculum improvement. Others in our society have the right and obligation to debate what our schools and curriculum ought to be. The state must assure its citizens that your students are achieving the fundamental skills and abilities that enable them to be productive, participating, well-adjusted citizens, now and in the future. The district must assure the school board that all students in the district are experiencing the best possible education. Parents must be assured that their children are receiving the kind of education they expect your school to provide. Lay groups will lobby to get their ideas for curriculum content and materials in line with their ideals and expectations. Educational researchers will report new knowledge and ideas

that may become important bases for improving your curriculum. There will be many participants in the curriculum improvement process, and your faculty must remain cognizant of these sometimes competing expectations and demands. To ignore them is to court disaster and to neglect important sources of ideas for curriculum improvement. Be aware of such expectations, examine them carefully at your school, and incorporate those that will improve the curriculum you want for your students.

These eight recommendations for your current and future efforts should enable you to maintain your curriculum improvement program as a way of life, not as an occasional response when your school comes under attack for needing improvement. Ideas will come and go, but the need to improve schools will be an ongoing one in a world that is experiencing tumultuous changes.

CONCLUSION

The process of curriculum improvement at your school will not be easy. Obstacles will be encountered along the way, people will disagree as to what ought to be changed, the magnitude of the tasks involved in improving schools will be overwhelming, energy needed in the change process will ebb and flow, and time and financial resources will never be in adequate supply. These limitations must be minimized, however, because curriculum improvement is an absolutely essential requirement if your school is to play the role in American society that we know it can and must. Change will not occur because some person or group at the federal, state, or even local level decrees it should. Curriculum improvement will occur only as a committed group of faculty and other interested parties at your school decides something can and should be done better and determines how to do it. All the pronouncements in the world will remain ineffectual until that commitment occurs.

Curriculum improvement is a process to be engaged in primarily by the local school staff and faculty. You deserve all the support that can possibly be mustered in order to improve the curriculum at your school. The challenge is great, but the results are worth all the struggles. Knowledge of the fundamental importance of schooling to your students should be enough to win and sustain your commitment to curriculum improvement. Your efforts to better your school today will have a major impact upon the future of our society and the ability of your students to create and maintain the kind of world they envision. Your work is that critical to the future.

APPENDIX
REFERENCES
INDEX
ABOUT THE AUTHOR

APPENDIX

A Study of Schooling:
General Description

A Study of Schooling was a 7-year study of a carefully selected group of schools. The purpose of the study was to determine what schooling was like in a sample of typical schools across the United States (Goodlad, Sirotnik, & Overman, 1979). A group of researchers studied schooling from a broad perspective encompassing many dimensions, rather than from a narrow in-depth focus on only one dimension. The school program, students' views of schooling, adults' views of schooling (teachers, administrators, and other professionals), and the relationship of the school to its community were studied in as much detail as was feasible. Questionnaires and observations were the primary sources of data, augmented by interviews and analyses of documents.

Schools were selected neither randomly nor for representativeness, but to correspond to a research matrix consisting of different types of schools: urban, suburban, and rural; small schools, medium schools, and large schools; largely white, largely minority, and racially mixed and ethnically diverse schools; and schools located in the Southeast, Southwest, Northwest, and central United States. Three schools were studied in each of the 13 communities selected: an elementary school that sent students to a junior high school which in turn sent students to a senior high school. The three feeder schools were referred to as a triple. Teams of trained data collectors lived in the communities for approximately one month as they collected the data. Their efforts were facilitated at all times by the researchers' central office staff, based in Los Angeles.

For over 1 year data were collected from 8,624 parents, 1,350 teachers, and over 17,000 students in 134 elementary classrooms and 369 junior high and 526 high school classes. Data were also collected from administrators, librarians, counselors, and other nonteaching, professional personnel. The amount of data thus collected, from a sample of this size and for a perspective this broad, was massive. Additional publications are available which report significant findings from various other aspects of the data not included in this book (e.g., Goodlad, 1984; Oakes, 1985; Sirotnik, 1983; B. Tye, 1985; K. Tye, 1985).

THE ELEMENTARY SCHOOL SAMPLE

The 13 elementary schools in the sample were the source of all the data reported in this book. Although all were elementary schools, there was a variety of organizational patterns and types of communities reflected in the sample. Eight of the elementary schools had a grade span from kindergarten through grade 6, five were kindergarten through grade 5. None of the kindergartens, however, was included as a part of the Study of Schooling sample, since not all states provide kindergarten as a part of the elementary school. Four of the schools were in urban communities, four were in rural/suburban communities, three were in rural areas, and two were in suburban communities.

Seven of the schools had a primarily white racial make-up, with white students accounting for 92% to 100% of the student population. Two schools had a predominantly Mexican-American composition, with one school being 66% Mexican-American and 34% white and the other school being 100% Mexican-American. Three schools had mixed student bodies; of these, one had whites, Orientals, blacks, and Mexican-Americans while the other two had approximately equal percentages of blacks and whites. One large urban school was virtually all black.

The schools ranged in student body size from 48 to 906; between the two extremes, two schools had enrollments in the 700s (745 and 701), two in the 600s (613 and 605), four in the 500s (598, 581, 521, and 513), and three in the 300s (340, 315, and 305). The median size student population total of all grades represented in the school was 581. The number of teachers ranged from 4 to 45, corresponding to the smallest and largest number of students. One school had 45 teachers, three had 30, one had 28, two had 24, three had 21, one had 18, one had 15, and one had four.

RESEARCH INSTRUMENTS

One major research instrument was an observation schedule specially developed for the study. Our trained observers spent two to three full days in selected classrooms in each of the schools, attending to carefully identified aspects of daily life. The resulting observations allowed us to obtain interactive data that significantly augmented our data collected by other means.

Questionnaires were the other major type of instrument for data collection. There were questionnaires for community members, parents, teachers, and students. Within the student instruments, some variation of the items was necessary to accommodate the different age levels of students. Thus, three different student questionnaires were developed, one for secondary students (grades 7–12), one for upper elementary students (grades 4–6), and one for early elementary students (grades 1–3). Each form of the questionnaire was developed with readability and familiarity with school as two major criteria. Elementary forms had to be easy for most students to read, in order to obtain needed comparable data throughout all the grade levels. Also, some questions asked of secondary students were thought to be too sophisticated or complex for elementary students to answer. These questions dealt with concepts that required more understanding of what schools were for and were like, for example. They required more insight about schooling than many elementary students were thought to possess, because of their more limited maturity and experience with schools.

Even within the elementary school, it was decided that the very young student would not be able to respond to some questions that upper elementary students could. This is why the two forms for the elementary school students were developed. Although they were similar in their intent and focus, some questions were presented differently between the two levels, and some questions were asked of upper elementary students that were not asked of early elementary students. The results of all these efforts were questionnaires that the research staff thought were appropriate and usable for each of the two age groups in the sample.

The teacher questionnaire was the same for all teachers, although a few sections were modified because of the organizational differences affecting teaching responsibilities from the elementary to the secondary schools. Teachers were asked many of the same questions that were asked of students; in addition, they were asked to provide extensive data about their demographic characteristics, classroom practices, and perceptions of the administration, as well as aspects of the total school and the community. The questionnaire was very detailed and required approximately one hour for a teacher to complete.

A questionnaire for parents was also included in the study. It was much less extensive than the ones for students and teachers, however, and focused primarily on the parents' general perceptions of the school their child attended; some demographic information was also requested.

References

Adler, Mortimer J. (1982). *The Paideia proposal: An educational manifesto.* New York: Macmillan.

Benham, Barbara J. (1978). *Curriculum materials analysis, by subject and by school.* Unpublished report, I/D/E/A, Los Angeles.

Benham, Barbara J. (1979). *Student life.* Unpublished paper from A Study of Schooling, I/D/E/A, Los Angeles.

Boyer, Ernest L. (1983). *High school: A report of the Carnegie Foundation for the Advancement of Teaching.* New York: Harper & Row.

A closer look at textbooks [entire issue]. (1985). *Educational Leadership, 43*(7).

Denham, Carolyn, & Ann Lieberman. (Eds.). (1980). *Time to learn.* Washington, DC: U.S. Department of Education and National Institute of Education.

Edmonds, Ronald R. (1982). Programs of school improvement: An overview. *Educational Leadership, 40*(3), 4–11.

Eisner, Elliot W. (1985). *The educational imagination: On the design and evaluation of school programs.* New York: Macmillan.

Eisner, Elliot W., & Elizabeth Vallance. (1974). *Conflicting conceptions of curriculum.* Berkeley: McCutchan.

Finn, Chester E., Jr. (1986). We can shape our destiny. *Educational Leadership, 44*(1), 4–6.

Fullan, Michael. (1982). *The meaning of educational change.* New York: Teachers College Press.

Giesen, Phillip, & Kenneth A. Sirotnik. (1979). *The methodology of classroom observation in A Study of Schooling* (I/D/E/A Study of Schooling Report No. 5). (ERIC Document Reproduction Service No. ED 214 875)

Goodlad, John I. (1975). *The dynamics of educational change: Toward responsive schools.* New York: McGraw-Hill.

Goodlad, John I. (1984). *A place called school: Prospects for the future.* New York: McGraw-Hill.

Goodlad, John I., M. Frances Klein, & associates. (1974). *Looking behind the classroom door.* Worthington, OH: Charles A. Jones.

Goodlad, John I., M. Frances Klein, & Kenneth A. Tye. (1979). The domains of curriculum and their study. In J. I. Goodlad and associates (Eds.), *Curric-*

ulum inquiry: The study of curriculum practice (pp. 43–76). New York: McGraw-Hill.

Goodlad, John I., Kenneth A. Sirotnik, & Bette C. Overman. (1979). A Study of Schooling: An overview. *Phi Delta Kappan, 60,* 174–178.

Goodlad, John I., with Renata Von Stoephasius & M. Frances Klein. (1966). *The changing school curriculum.* New York: The Fund for the Advancement of Education.

Griffin, Gary A. (1979). Levels of curricular decision-making. In J. I. Goodlad & associates (Eds.), *Curriculum inquiry: The study of curriculum practice* (pp. 77–100). New York: McGraw-Hill.

Hass, Glen. (1987). Who should plan the curriculum? In G. Hass (Ed.), *Planning: A new approach* (5th ed.) (pp. 326–329). Boston: Allyn and Bacon.

House, Ernest R. (1974). *The politics of educational innovation.* Berkeley: McCutchan.

Jackson, Phillip. (1968). *Life in classrooms.* New York: Holt, Rinehart & Winston.

Joyce, Bruce, & Marsha Weil. (1985). *Models of teaching.* Englewood Cliffs, NJ: Prentice-Hall.

Klein, M. Frances. (1980a). *State and district curriculum guides: One aspect of the formal curriculum* (I/D/E/A Study of Schooling Report No. 9). (ERIC Document Reproduction Service No. ED 214 879)

Klein, M. Frances (1980b). *Teacher perceived sources of influence on what is taught in subject areas* (I/D/E/A Study of Schooling Report No. 15). (ERIC Document Reproduction Service No. ED 214 885)

Klein, M. Frances. (1983). *How to study a school.* West Lafayette, IN: Kappa Delta Pi.

Klein, M. Frances. (1986). Alternative curriculum conceptions and designs. *Theory Into Practice, 25*(1), 31–35.

Klein, M. Frances. (1987, April 20–24). *State legislated curriculum: Assessing the impact of the shift in locus of authority. Interpretation from the perspective of a curriculum theorist.* Paper presented at the annual meeting of the American Educational Research Association, Washington, DC.

Komoski, P. Kenneth. (1978). The realities of choosing and using instructional materials. *Educational Leadership, 36*(1), 46–50.

Lieberman, Ann, & Lynne Miller. (1984). *Teachers, their world, and their work.* Alexandria, VA: Association for Supervision and Curriculum Development.

Longstreet, Wilma. (1982). Action research: A paradigm. *The Educational Forum, 56*(2), 135–158.

Lortie, Dan C. (1975). *School-teacher: A sociological study.* Chicago: University of Chicago Press.

McLaughlin, Milbrey W., & David D. Marsh. (1978). Staff development and school change. *Teachers College Record, 80*(4), 69–94.

McNeil, John D. (1985). *Curriculum: A comprehensive introduction.* Boston: Little, Brown.

National Commission on Excellence in Education. (1983). *A nation at risk.* Washington, DC: U.S. Department of Education.

Oakes, Jeannie. (1985). *Keeping track: How schools structure inequality.* New Haven: Yale University Press.

Overly, Norman. (1970). *The unstudied curriculum.* Washington, DC: Association for Supervision and Curriculum Development.

Overman, Bette C. (1980a). *Functions of schooling: Perceptions and preferences of teachers, parents, and students* (I/D/E/A Study of Schooling Report No. 10). (ERIC Document Reproduction Service No. ED 214 880)

Overman, Bette C. (1980b). *Variety and intensity of school-related problems as perceived by teachers, parents, and students* (I/D/E/A Study of Schooling Report No. 17). (ERIC Document Reproduction Service No. ED 214 887)

Pinar, William. (Ed.). (1975). *Curriculum theorizing: The reconceptualists.* Berkeley: McCutchan.

Raths, James D. (1971). Teaching without specific objectives. *Educational Leadership, 28*(7), 714–720.

Sanders, Donald P., & Marian Schwab. (1981). *Annehurst: The natural history of a good school.* West Lafayette, IN: Kappa Delta Pi.

Sarason, Seymour B. (1982). *The culture of the school and the problem of change* (2nd ed.). Boston: Allyn and Bacon.

Sirotnik, Kenneth A. (1981). *What you see is what you get: A summary of observations in over 1,000 elementary and secondary classrooms* (I/D/E/A Study of Schooling Report No. 29). (ERIC Document Reproduction Service No. ED 214 897)

Sirotnik, Kenneth A. (1983). What you see is what you get: Consistency, persistency, and mediocracy in classrooms. *Harvard Educational Review, 53,* 16–31.

Sirotnik, Kenneth A. (1987). *The school as the center of change* (Occasional Paper No. 5). Seattle: University of Washington, Center for Educational Renewal.

Sizer, Theodore R. (1984). *Horace's compromise: The dilemma of the American high school.* Boston: Houghton Mifflin.

Tye, Barbara J. (1985). *Multiple realities: A study of 13 American high schools.* Lanham, MD: University Press of America.

Tye, Kenneth A. (1979a). *Teacher perception of the appropriateness of content and materials.* Unpublished report, I/D/E/A, Los Angeles.

Tye, Kenneth A. (1979b). *Teacher perception of information utilized in individualizing instruction.* Unpublished report, I/D/E/A, Los Angeles.

Tye, Kenneth A. (1979c). *Teacher perception of means of individualizing instruction.* Unpublished report, I/D/E/A, Los Angeles.

Tye, Kenneth A. (1979d). *Teacher perception of use and value of behaviorally stated objectives.* Unpublished report, I/D/E/A, Los Angeles.

Tye, Kenneth A. (1979e). *Teacher report of time expected of students on homework.* Unpublished report, I/D/E/A, Los Angeles.

Tye, Kennetn A. (1979f). *Teacher report of time spent on planning and preparing materials.* Unpublished report, I/D/E/A, Los Angeles.

Tye, Kenneth A. (1979g). *Teacher report of the use of behaviorally stated objectives.* Unpublished report, I/D/E/A, Los Angeles.

Tye, Kenneth A. (1979h). *Teacher satisfaction with areas of teaching and planning.* Unpublished report, I/D/E/A, Los Angeles.

Tye, Kenneth A. (1980). *Changing our schools: The realities* (I/D/E/A Study of Schooling Report No. 30). (ERIC Document Reproduction Service No. ED 218 241)

Tye, Kenneth A. (1985). *The junior high: School in search of a mission.* Lanham, MD: University Press of America.

Tye, Kenneth A., & Jerrold M. Novotney. (1975). *Schools in transition: The practitioner as change agent.* New York: McGraw-Hill.

Vallance, Elizabeth. (1973/74). Hiding the hidden curriculum: An interpretation of the language of justification in nineteenth century educational reform. *Curriculum Theory Network, 4*(1), 5–22.

Wise, Arthur E. (1979). *Legislated learning.* Berkeley: University of California Press.

Wise, Arthur E., & Linda Darling-Hammond. (1984/85). Teacher evaluation and teacher professionalism. *Educational Leadership, 42*(4), 28–31.

Wright, David P. (1980a). *Teachers' educational beliefs* (I/D/E/A Study of Schooling Report No. 14). (ERIC Document Reproduction Service No. ED 214 884)

Wright, David P. (1980b). *Teachers' perceptions of their own influence over school policies and decisions* (I/D/E/A Study of Schooling Report No. 16). (ERIC Document Reproduction Service No. ED 214 886)

Wright, Joyce E. (1980a). *Teaching and learning* (I/D/E/A Study of Schooling Report No. 18). (ERIC Document Reproduction Service No. ED 214 888)

Wright, Joyce E. (1980b). *The role and status of elementary arts programs* (I/D/E/A Study of Schooling Report No. 21). (ERIC Document Reproduction Service No. ED 186 338)

Zahorik, John A. (1976). The virtue of vagueness in instructional objectives. *Elementary School Journal, 76,* 411–419.

Index

Academic learning time (ALT)
  classroom practices and, 79–82
  in school and classroom contexts, 122
Acquired Immune Deficiency Syndrome
  (AIDS), 171–172
Action research, 0
Adler, Mortimer J., 1
Administrators
  classroom practices and, 65–66, 79
  classroom quality of life and, 165–166
  intended curriculum and, 23, 33, 42–44
  process and substance of curriculum
    reform and, 1, 8, 10
  and school and classroom contexts,
    118–119
  teachers as professional educators and,
    143–145
Audio-visual (A-V) materials, 70–72, 75,
  82

Behavioral objectives
  classroom practices and, 51–54, 65–68,
    80
  classroom quality of life and, 153–154,
    156, 160, 165, 168
  impact of teachers and, 136, 138
Benham, Barbara J., 29, 116
Boyer, Ernest L., vii, 1

Change, 40
  establishing core group for, 9
  factors affecting implementation of, 8–9
  organizing for, 5–9
  process of, 7–9
  substance of, 5–7
  time consumed by, 174
Classrooms, 46–82
  advanced technology in, 120–121

appropriateness of learning materials
  and content in, 76–78
attitudes toward curriculum and, 92–93
continued professional growth of
  teachers and, 131–133
curriculum decision making and, 86–88,
  98–100
education beliefs of teachers and,
  140–142
how time is spent in, 47–55, 78
impact of teachers and, 135–142
instructional practices in, 55–62
intended curriculum and, 25–26, 29,
  35–37, 40–44, 46–48, 50–51, 62,
  76, 78–82
people and groupings in, 109–111,
  121–122
physical context of, 105–108
process and substance of curriculum
  reform and, 2, 4–6, 8–10
professional preparation of teachers
  and, 128
quality of life in, 146–170
rationale and methodology for
  evaluation of, 147–150
social context of, 105–106, 108–117
teachers as professional educators and,
  143–144
types of activities in, 69–76, 78, 80
use of learning principles in, 62–69
Community, 81
  as curriculum improvement resource, 174
  establishing base in, 9
  intended curriculum and, 15, 43
  process and substance of curriculum
    reform and, 5, 9
  teachers as professional educators and,
    145

Computers, 28, 41, 120
Core groups, establishment of, 9
Curriculum. *See also* Explicit curriculum;
        Implicit curriculum; Intended
        curriculum
    attitudes toward, 85, 91–98, 102–103
    broad view of, 22–23
    comprehensive examination of, 6
    definitions of, 13–14, 46
    developing systematic approach to, 7
Curriculum guides, 67
    analysis of, 24–29, 33
    content in, 26, 34–37
    decision making and, 85–86, 88, 99
    evaluation and, 26–27
    goals and objectives of, 24–26
    individualization and, 27, 36
    intended curriculum and, 15, 24–29,
        33–39
    traditional roles reflected in, 28
Curriculum reform
    guidelines for, 172–176
    history of, 1–2
    importance of, 172
    recurrent demands for, 3–4, 171–172
    resistance to, 2

Darling-Hammond, Linda, 144
Decision making, 83–91
    classroom quality of life and, 148,
        155–156, 162–165, 168
    influences on curriculum and, 85–91
    issues in, 97–104
Denham, Carolyn, 51, 61–62, 79, 122
Dropouts, 98, 171–172
    curriculum and, 102–104
Drug and alcohol abuse, 139

Early elementary students
    aspects of classroom life for, 148–156,
        166, 168–170
    satisfactory classrooms defined by, 166,
        168–170
Edmonds, Ronald R., 84
Educational emphases, 15–23, 33, 39. *See
    also specific educational emphases*
    actual importance of, 17
    broad curriculum view support for,
        22–23
    desirability of, 18–19
    keeping open mind on, 21–22

    most desirable, 19–21
    most pursued, 19
Educational Leadership, 89
Educational publications, 132, 143,
        173–174
Eisner, Elliot W., 13–14, 66–67, 69, 105,
        120, 137
Engagement, active vs. passive, 60
Explicit curriculum, 7
    continued professional growth of
        teachers and, 133
    and school and classroom contexts,
        105–106, 108–109, 111, 115–116,
        120–121

Finn, Chester E., Jr., 88
Fullan, Michael, 7

Giesen, Phillip, 71
Goodlad, John I., vii–ix, xii, 1–4, 7,
        40–41, 46, 84–85, 88, 111, 125, 147,
        179–180
Griffin, Gary A., 84
Grouping patterns, 109–111, 121–122

Hass, Glen, 102
Homework, time spent on, 50–51
House, Ernest R., viii

Implicit curriculum
    challenging tradition and, 119–123
    classroom quality of life and, 169
    continued professional growth of
        teachers and, 132–133
    paying attention to, 6–7
    personal characteristics of teachers and,
        126
    potential messages of, 117–119
    power of, 117–123
    and school and classroom contexts,
        105–107, 109, 111–112, 115–123
Individualization
    classroom life for early elementary
        students and, 153–154, 156
    classroom life for upper elementary
        students and, 162
    classroom practices and, 67–69
    intended curriculum and, 27, 36, 41–43
    and school and classroom contexts,
        110–111, 120
Intellectual development, 97

classroom quality of life and, 161
intended curriculum and, 15–22, 25
Intended curriculum, 13–45
  and analysis of curriculum guides,
    24–29
  classroom practices and, 25–26, 29,
    35–37, 40–44, 46–48, 50–51, 62,
    76, 78–82
  curriculum decision making and, 88
  issues to consider in, 38–45
  monitoring of, 174–175
  political importance of, 46
  and selection of content and learning
    materials, 29–34
  and sources of influence over content,
    34–38
  and surveying educative functions of
    schooling, 14–23

Jackson, Phillip, 105, 111
Joyce, Bruce, 109

Klein, M. Frances, 2, 4, 8, 14, 24, 34,
  39–40, 83–84, 86, 88, 99
Komoski, P. Kenneth, 76

Labor unions, 137, 143, 163
Learning materials and content
  appropriateness of, 76–78
  classroom practices and, 62–69, 75–78,
    81–82
  classroom quality of life and, 160, 163
  curriculum decision making and, 88–90
  intended curriculum and, 26, 29–38,
    40–43
  satisfactory classrooms and, 167
  sources of influence over, 34–38
Lecturing, demonstrating, and explaining,
  56
Lieberman, Ann, 51, 61–62, 79, 122, 133,
  144
Literacy, meaning of, 171–172
Long-range plans, development of, 11
Longstreet, Wilma, 8
Lortie, Dan C., 133, 137, 144

McLaughlin, Milbrey, 2, 7, 84–85
McNeil, John D., 13
Marsh, David D., 2, 7, 84–85
Meetings, organizing of, 10
Miller, Lynne, 133, 144

Minority groups
  intended curriculum and, 21–22
  personal characteristics of teachers and,
    126
  in Study of Schooling sample, 180
Momentum, maintaining of, 9–11

National Commission on Excellence in
  Education, 1
Nation at Risk, A, vii
Novotney, Jerrold M., 2, 7

Oakes, Jeannie, 180
Observation schedules, 180
Observing and monitoring, 56
Overly, Norman, 105
Overman, Bette C., 17–18, 91, 125, 179

Parents, 80
  attitudes toward curriculum of, 85,
    91–92, 96–98
  curriculum decision making and, 80,
    101
  curriculum improvement involvement
    of, 174–175
  impact of teachers and, 136, 138–139
  intended curriculum and, 15–23, 25, 33,
    37, 39
  process and substance of curriculum
    reform and, 9
  teachers as professional educators and,
    144
Personal development, 97
  classroom quality of life and, 161
  educational beliefs of teachers and, 142
  intended curriculum and, 15–20, 22, 25,
    39, 82
Pinar, William, 13
Professional organizations, 131, 143

Questioning, 56–57
Questionnaires, 181

Raths, James D., 66
Research, xi–xiv, 171
  action, 8
  on attitudes toward curriculum, 92–95,
    97
  on classroom practices, 46–48, 51–52,
    55–77, 79–80
  on classroom quality of life, 146–170

Research (*continued*)
    on curriculum decision making, 87–89,
        98–100
    curriculum improvement involvement
        of, 175–176
    intended curriculum and, 15–26, 28–29,
        32–33, 36–41, 43
    process and substance of curriculum
        reform and, 2–3, 8, 10
    role of, xii–xiv
    on school and classroom contexts, 107,
        109–111, 114–115, 119
    on teachers, 124–132, 134–135, 138–143
Role playing, 74–75, 82
Routines, 160
    classroom time spent on, 51–55, 59–60

Sanders, Donald P., 137
Sarason, Seymour B., viii
Schools, schooling
    attitudes toward curriculum and, 91–92,
        97–98
    classroom practices and, 47–49, 51–54,
        60–62, 68, 75, 79–82
    classroom quality of life and, 147,
        149–150, 152–153, 157, 161–162,
        165, 167–169
    continued professional growth of
        teachers and, 130–134
    curriculum decision making and, 83–84,
        86, 88, 90, 98, 101–102
    deciding what is desirable for, 60–62
    dropout problem of, 102–103
    educational beliefs of teachers and,
        140–142
    impact of teachers and, 135–142
    intended curriculum and, 14–24, 26–27,
        29–30, 32–34, 36–43, 45, 46
    management-and-labor model of,
        136–137
    mission of, 173
    monitoring practices of, 174–175
    personal characteristics of teachers and,
        126–127, 135
    physical context of, 105–108
    process and substance of curriculum
        reform and, 1–12
    professional preparation of teachers
        and, 128
    social context of, 105–106, 108–117

    surveying educative functions of, 14–23
    teachers as professional educators and,
        144–145
Schwab, Marian, 137
Short-range plans, development of, 11
Sirotnik, Kenneth A., viii, 55, 71, 107,
        125, 179–180
Sizer, Theodore R., vii
Social development, 97
    educational beliefs of teachers and, 142
    intended curriculum and, 15–20, 22, 25,
        39, 81–82
Social interactions, 111–115, 170
Society, 103
    educational beliefs and, 141–142
    intended curriculum and, 24–26, 39–41
    mission of schools and, 173
    process and substance of curriculum
        reform and, 1–2
    teachers as professional educators and,
        144
Students
    attitudes toward curriculum of, 85,
        91–97, 102–103
    attitudes toward other students of,
        160–161
    classroom practices and, 46–47, 49–78,
        80–82
    classroom quality of life and, 146–170
    continued professional growth of
        teachers and, 130–131, 133–134
    curriculum decision making and, 83–91,
        97, 100–102
    dropouts among, 98, 102–104
    educational beliefs of teachers and,
        140–142
    feedback to, 63–64, 80
    impact of teachers and, 136–138,
        140–142
    intended curriculum and, 13–17, 19–29,
        32–36, 38–45
    in listening to other students, 70, 75
    mission of schools and, 173
    personal characteristics of teachers and,
        126–127, 129, 135
    process and substance of curriculum
        reform and, 1–2, 4, 6–10
    professional preparation of teachers
        and, 128–129
    responding to, 57–58

and school and classroom contexts, 105–123
self-concepts of, 115–117
social interactions among, 113–115
social interactions between teachers and, 112–113, 170
teachers as professional educators and, 145
Study of Schooling, A, xi–xiii, 10, 48, 66, 100, 107, 143
classroom quality of life and, 146–147, 166
general description of, 179–181
intended curriculum and, 14–15, 28–29, 34, 38
Subject areas
attitudes toward, 92–97, 103
classroom practices and, 48–50, 66–67, 70–78, 82
classroom quality of life and, 151–154, 157–163
classroom time allocated to, 48–50
continued professional growth of teachers and, 130–132
curriculum decision making in, 89
educational beliefs of teachers and, 141
impact of teachers and, 138, 141
intended curriculum and, 29–35, 42
professional preparation of teachers and, 127–129
satisfactory classrooms and, 166–169
and school and classroom contexts, 108
time spent by teachers preparing for, 50

Teachers, teaching, 65, 124–145
attitudes toward curriculum and, 85, 91–95, 97–98
career satisfaction and, 134–135, 143
classroom practices and, 46–82
classroom quality of life and, 146, 148–150, 152–170
curriculum decision making and, 84–88, 90, 97–102
dropout problem and, 102–104
encouraging spirit of inquiry in, 175
expectations of others and, 175–176
impact on professional milieu of, 135–142
intended curriculum and, 13–45, 46
listening to, 69–70, 75, 80

new roles for, 43–45
opportunities for continued professional growth of, 129–134, 143–144, 174
personal characteristics of, 125–127, 129, 134–135
process and substance of curriculum reform and, 1–12
as professional educators, 142–145
professional preparation of, 127–129, 143, 162, 170
and school and classroom contexts, 105–115, 118–122
social interactions between students and, 112–113, 170
Testing
classroom practices and, 49, 68, 74–75, 82
educational beliefs of teachers and, 141
intended curriculum and, 26–27, 30–34, 36, 39
Textbooks
classroom practices and, 77–78
curriculum decision making and, 84, 86, 99
intended curriculum and, 30–32, 34–37, 39, 42–43
Theory and practice, 6, 23, 142
Tradition, challenging of, 119–123
Tye, Barbara J., 180
Tye, Kenneth A., 2, 7, 50, 66–68, 84, 92, 126, 132, 134, 180

Upper elementary students, 148–150, 156–170

Vallance, Elizabeth, 13–14, 105
Vocational development, 97, 161
intended curriculum and, 15–22, 25, 39, 81–82
Von Stoephasius, Renata, 2

Weil, Marsha, 169
Wise, Arthur E., viii, 144
Workshops, 130–131, 143
Wright, David P., 136, 140
Wright, Joyce E., 48, 52–53, 57, 63, 70, 73–74, 87–88, 92, 94, 107, 109–110, 112, 114, 127, 130

Zahorik, John A., 66–67

About the Author

Dr. M. FRANCES KLEIN is Professor at the University of Southern California and holds the Robert Naslund Endowed Chair in Curriculum Theory. She is active as an educational researcher, is a frequent presenter at educational conferences, and is a member of many professional organizations. She was the chairperson of the curriculum subsection of A Study of Schooling, on which this book is based. Consulting activities bring her in frequent contact with schools, colleges, governmental agencies at all levels, and publishing companies. Her extensive publications include books, monographs, encyclopedia articles, and contributions to professional journals.